Historical Sketches of the Ancient Negro

A Compilation

I0804247

Historical Sketches of the Ancient Negro

A Compilation

Edward E. Carlisle
and Josephine E. Carlisle

Black Classic Press
Baltimore

Historical Sketches of the Ancient Negro

Copyright 1920
Josephine E. Carlisle

Published 2004
Black Classic Press

Introduction copyright 1981
Dr. G. K. Osei

All Rights Reserved.

Library of Congress Card Catalog Number: 2004101940

ISBN 1-58073-017-5

Cover design by Michelle D. Wright

We would like to acknowledge the late G. K. Osei for first republishing this text in 1981.

Founded in 1978, Black Classic Press specializes in bringing to ligh
obscure and significant works by and about people of African descent
If our books are not available in your area, ask your local bookseller t
order them. Our current list of titles can be obtained by writing:

Black Classic Press
c/o List
P.O. Box 13414
Baltimore, MD 21203
www.blackclassic.com

INTRODUCTION — Dr. G.K. Osei L.L.B., L.L.M., Ph.D.

Africa has been an object of interest to all honest people in every age, as the birth-place of civilization, art, science, and religion. Many of the virtues taught by Christianity and Judaism are the ideal of the ancient Africans. Quite unfortunately, most of our information about the history of Africa comes from the white missionaries and colonial ambassadors who gave, in some cases, wrong account of actual occurrences and twisted things out of their context. They gave an unbalanced view of the whole situation. A history of a nation must be written by the natives who are in a better position to fully understand the minds of the people and put correct interpretation and emphasis on historical events. Africa has a glorious past of which we are all proud of and which no amount of hate and prejudice can efface from history. In reconstructing Africa let us relive the past and draw inspiration from it.

The aim of the authors *(Historical Sketches of the Ancient Negro)* was to show to the world some of the great Africans who played their parts in the history of the world. They compiled their book from the works of historians who were bold enough to mention Africans in their works. Some of the Africans mentioned in this book are Thotimoses III, Queen Tyi, Hannibal, Amenophis III, and IV, Aahmes, Severus Sercus and some of the Pharaohs who ruled Egypt and Ethiopia.

Pharaoh Aahmes was the founder of the Eighteenth Dynasty; and it was he who drove the Hyksos out of Egypt. What were the results of the expulsion of the Hyksos from Egypt? The period after the expulsion of the invaders was very remarkable. Aahmes became the master of the whole of Egypt. From this period until the conquest of the country by the Ethiopians, Egypt was a single country. It was during this period that Egyptian art attained its highest perfection. The great temples of Thebes were also built. Egypt became an Empire and Ethiopia, India, Syria and Mesopotamia were invaded and added to the empire. During the nineteenth dynasty Egypt reached her highest pitch of greatness, internal and external.

Each district in Egypt had its own god. Amon was the god of Thebes. With the expulsion of the Hyksos, Amon became the main god of Egypt. After the overthrow of the Hyksos it was no longer possible for the Pharaohs to refer to themselves as the *lords of the two Egypts.* Egypt had become an empire and the Pharaohs were the lords of the other lands. It must be mentioned here that almost all the Pharaohs after the expulsion were soldiers. The brave, resolute and skilful generals of Egypt are to be found in the 18th Dynasty. Aahmes was brave, active, energetic, liberal, beloved by his subjects. The two landmarks in Egyptian history were the unification of the two lands under Menes and the expulsion of the Hyksos.

Amenophis III reigned for a long time peacefully. It was after his reign that Amenophis IV mounted the throne of the Empire. Amenophis IV deserted the god Amon and made Aten to become the national god. Amenophis had hoped to govern Egypt by an idea, a dream, but an empire, however benevolently administered, must be defended and protected by force. Amenophis lost his empire without a fight. The succession of weak pharaohs caused the power of Egypt to decline.

Ethiopia with its power conquered Egypt. Tarakus was a warlike Pharaoh who led his army against Sennacherib, King of Asyria and defeated him. Because of Psammetichus' favours to the Greeks to settle in Egypt in the seventh century B.C., two hundred and fifty thousand Egyptian soldiers migrated to Ethiopia. They were settled at the extreme southern part of Ethiopia.

Many of the sovereigns of Ethiopia were queens. In 20 B.C., a queen called Candace made war against Augustus Caesar. During the reign of another Candace the Jewish religion prevailed in Ethiopia. The confidential adviser of the queen went to Jerusalem to worship and returned in 53 A.D. It was this adviser who introduced Christianity into Ethiopia. It is said that he was converted to Christianity by St. Philips. Why is it that Ethiopia is mentioned more in the Bible than Egypt? It is because at the time the Bible was written the Ethiopian Pharaohs were wearing the Double Crown of Egypt. Most of the Bible writters lived during this period.

The ancient Ethiopians built wonderful obelisks, sphinxes, monuments and colossal statues, rock-cut temples just like their brothers in Egypt. Their sepulchers show the greatest purity of taste. The vases of Ethiopia as shown on the monuments, show a taste and elegance of form that has never been surpassed. "In sculpture and coloring, the edifices of Meroe, though less profusely adorned, rival the best specimens of Egyptian art."

The rock temple of Ipsambul, near Derr is the most wonderful of all the monuments of Nubia. The temple is cut from a mountain of solid rock, adorned inside with colossi statues and painted sculptures, representing castles, battles, triumphal processions and religious pagents. On the outside are four colossis, larger than any sculptured figures in Egypt, except the Sphinx. One of these colossi is sixty-five feet high. This temple is one hundred and seventy feet in depth, and contains fourteen apartments one of which is fifty-seven feet by fifty-two, and is supported by images with folded arms, thirty feet high. The rock in which this temple is built is six hundred feet in height.

Meroe played an important part in the ancient caravan trade. It was the emporium of trade between the north and the south, between the east and the west. The fertility of its soil helped the Ethiopians to buy luxuries with native products. Fabrics were woven in Meroe and the manufacturers of metal were here as flourishing as in Egypt.

Meroe was almost surrounded with rivers, and it was a center of trade. The ivory, ebony and spices from Central Africa to Egypt passed though Meroe. Trade with India was conducted from the harbors of Meroe. This great city flourished about 1000 B.C. and held Upper Egypt. This does not mean that its civilization started in 1000 B.C. "The great changes in the lines of trade, the ravages of successive conquereors and revolutions, the fanaticism of the Saracens, and the ruin of the fertile soil by the moving sands of the desert, together with the pressure of nomadic herds, all contributed to the extinction of this powerful ancient empire (Ethiopia)."

November 6, 1981

PREFACE

We have endeavored to present to our readers a selected collection of historical facts in one volume on the Ethiopian or Ancient Negro. It has long since been conceded that Negro nations or Hamites were the earliest civilized peoples and the real source of the civilization we enjoy to-day. More and more are we made cognizant of the fact that men to-day are but doing over the things that were done thousands of years ago and it is interesting to note that the Negro's share in those early activities was not a small one. It is to familiarize the youth as well as the adult of the Negro race with the events in which many of their ancestors centered that it may be an incentive to higher aims and nobler aspirations.

"Now our day is come," says one writer, "we have been born out of the eternal silence; and now we will live for ourselves and not as the pall bearers of a funeral. Now that we are here we will put our own interpretation on things and our own things for interpretation." This has been our chief aim in compiling this work — to interpret the Negro's status in the ancient world unbiased and impartial — to emphasize his identity in the midst of the Caucasian chaos in which most historians have placed him — only as a hewer of stone and drawer of water is he in bold relief. Our own interpretation has preserved to us, however, many glowing accounts of the deeds of black men with which every one of African descent should be familiar and justly proud. J. E. C.

CONTENTS.

and their children Hashep and Hatasu. Thotmes II and Thotmes III, Amenophis II, Thotmes IV, Amenophis III (Mimnon), Amenophis IV.

VI.

How Moses made war upon the Ethiopians. His marriage with the Ethiopian Princess Tharbis.

VII.

How Moses fled out of Egypt into Midian. He marries Zipporah an Ethiopian woman.

VIII.

Moses receives Jethro, his father-in-law — the black priest of Midian who organized the first court of equity.

IX.

THE QUEEN OF SHEBA.

X.

Carthage.

Hamilcar, Hannibal, Hasdrubal, The Punic Wars, Hannibals Treaty.

XI.

Septimus Severeus, Negro Emperor of Rome. His Sons, Geta and Caracalla.

Earth had mighty dark hued heroes
  In the morning of the world
Giant warriors clad in lightning
  Who their bold defiance hurled
High as heaven and down the ages:
  Nimrod Seti, Rameses,
Hannibal — bold lions rampant
  Romping through dawn's amethyst—
Bronzed Nemeans, leaping storming
  Down the morning's amber mist!

Rise, forgotten Past! Meroë
  Where great Moses loved arise!
Tyre Thebes Nineveh we knew you
  When the world was paradise!
Sphinxes, pyramids, silent Memnon
  Ruined Memphis — Babylon,
Relics of great deeds and empires
  Of the proud, dark peoples gone,
We your clay creators loved you
  In the clanging purple dawn.

Rev. Dr. Jas. D. Corrothers.

THE DISPERSION OF THE HUMAN FAMILY.

After the deluge the earth was divided between the three sons of Noah, Japhet, Shem and Ham. The peoples connected with Japhet occupy the northern portion of the known world and include the Madai (Medes) on the East of Assyria, Javans, Ionians, i. e. Greeks, on the West Coast of Asia Minor and Tarshish (Tartessus) on the West Coast of Spain.

Shem is the ancestor of several peoples, occupying roughly speaking, the central portion of the known world. Shem stands for a people in Palestine or some portion of them with whom Japhet lived in close conjunction and to whom Canaan was subjugated.[1]

Ham's descendants were alloted the southern portion and possessed the land from Syria and Amans and the mountains of Libanus seizing upon all that was on its seacoasts and as far as the ocean, and keeping it as their own. (Josephus.)

"According to Armenian tradition to Ham was given the region of the blacks, to Shem the region of the tawny, *fuscorum* and to Japhet the region of the ruddy, *rubrorum*. To the sons of Shem was allotted the middle of the earth, viz. — Palestine, Syria, Assyria, Samaria, Singar (or Shinar), Babel (or Babylonia), Persia and Higiaz (Arabia); to the sons of Ham Tiemen or Idumea (Jer. 49:7) Africa, Nigritia, Egypt, Nubia, Ethiopia, Scindia and India (or India west and east of the river

[1] A. H. M'Neil, Bib. Dict.

Indus); to the sons of Japhet also, Garbia (the north), Spain, France, the the countries of the Greeks, Sclavonians, Bulgarians, Turks and Armenians."[1]

Ham, or Cham, son of Noah and brother to Shem and Japhet is believed to be Noah's youngest son. Ham, says Dr. Hales, signifies burnt or black and this name was peculiarly significant of the regions allotted to his family. To the Cushites, or children of his eldest son Cush were allotted the hot southern regions of Asia along the coasts of the Persian Gulf, Suisiana, Chusistan Arabia, etc.; to the sons Canaan, Palestine and Syria; to the sons of Mizraim Egypt and Lybia Libya in Africa.[2]

THE SONS OF HAM.

The first and most celebrated of Ham's sons was Cush who gave name to the land of Cush both in Asia and Africa, the former called Chusistan by the Arabian Geographers, Suisiana by the Greeks, Cusha Dwipa within by the Hindus, the other Cusha Dwipa without.

The posterity of Cush spread over a great part of Asia and Africa, were called Cushim or Cushites by the Greeks and Romans and in our Bible Ethiopians. They first settled on the Gulf of Persia, spread over India and Arabia, particularly its western part on the Red Sea, invaded Egypt under the name of Hyksos or Shepherd kings and after ruling Egypt for five centuries passed into Central Africa and first peopled the countries

[1] Fessenden & Co's. Ency.
[2] Watson, Fessenden & Co's. Ency.

south of Egypt, Nubia, Abyssinian and other countries farther south.[1]

And Cush begat Nimrod "he began to be mighty hunter in the earth." (*Gen.*) and the most conspicuous Negro character of early antiquity. He was the indirect cause of the dispersion of mankind over the earth, being one of the first examples of God's use of man as an agent in carrying out the divine purpose. Having great influence over the people, he suggested the building of a tower that should reach to heaven and make them a name and also serve as a refuge should there be another flood. To this the people readily agreed and proceeded to carry out Nimrod's rebellious plans, but were suddenly confused, not being able to understand one another, and the tower, called Babel (confusion) was abandoned. God punished them in this way because they had been drawn away from their allegiance to Him.

He may be styled the parent of organized human society. "He, Nimrod, first subverted the patriarchal government and introduced the Zabian idolatry or worship of the heavenly host; and after his death, was deified by his subjects, and supposed to be translated into the constellations of Orion attended by his hounds Sirius and Canicular, and still pursuing his favorite game, the great bear."[2]

Nimrod was a despot and ruled tyrannically but we can hardly conceive of any other form of government being adequate for the horde with which he had to contend, beset with doubts and fears. That Nimrod did

[1] Fessenden & Co's. Ency.
[2] Watson, Fessenden & Co's. Ency.

not follow his kindred, but remained in the land of Shinar, a usurper, but tends to show that God had work to be done and had chosen whom he thought best fitted to perform it. From Nimrod we trace the Asiatic Ethiopians and those of India.

Canaan the fourth son of Ham settled what was known in patriarchal ages as India and called it from his own name Canaan. The posterity of Canaan was numerous. His eldest son Sidon founded the city of Sidon and was father of the Sidonians and Phoenicians notwithstanding the curse (Gen. 9:25) is directed against Canaan the son and not against the father, it is often supposed that all the posterity of Ham were placed under this maladiction, "Cursed be Canaan a servant of servants shall he be unto his brethren." But the true reason why Canaan only was mentioned probably is that the curse was in fact restricted to the posterity of Canaan. It is true that many Africans of other branches of Ham's family have been cruelly enslaved; but so have other tribes in different parts of the world. There is certainly no proof that the Negro race was placed under this malediction.

Whatever punishment the Canaanites received was due to their disobedience and sins. "Joshua extirpated great numbers and obliged the rest to fly, some of them into Africa, and others into Greece. Procopius says, they first retreated into Egypt, but advanced into Africa where they built many cities, and spread themselves over these vast regions which reach to the straits, preserving their old language with little alteration. In the time of Athanasius, (296) the Africans still said they were descended from the Canaanites; and when asked their origin, they answered, "Canaani."

It is agreed that the Punic tongue was nearly the same as the Canaanitish or Hebrew.[1]

Now all the children of Mizraim, being eight in number, possessed the land from Gaza to Egypt though it retained the name of one only, the Philistim, for the Greeks called part of that country Palestine. As for the rest we know nothing of them besides their names; for the *Ethiopic war* caused those cities to be overthrown. Phut was the founder of Libya and called the inhabitants Phutites from himself. (Josephus.)

Thus we see that many centuries of time elapsed before these peoples arrived at fixed or final places of abode from a geographical point of view. The children of Ham were the leading people at this early period. 'Their early possession of the seacoasts made them a seafaring race and early established commercial intercourse between them, thus enabling them to sooner arrive at civilization and the luxuries of life than their simpler pastoral brethren of the other two families. Tyre, Sidon and Carthage were early distinguished for their commerce, but the sooner fell into decay.'

State of Meroë.

Let the mighty men come forth; the Ethiopians that handle the shield. —*Jer. XLVI*, 9.

The Ethiopians were a civilized people who dwelt in cities; — who erected temples and other edifices; who though without letters, had hieroglyphics; who had government and laws; and the fame of whose

[1] Watson, Fessenden & Co's. Ency.

progress in knowledge and the social arts spread in the earliest ages over a considerable part of the earth.

Meroë the mother city and capital of all Ethiopia has been celebrated for upwards of two thousand years, but its distant situation has always involved it in mystery and obscurity. It was brought to light by Burkhardt and Caillaud Meroë, however, did not appear alone; a new world of antiquities was laid open to the view of the astonished spectator.

The southern boundary of Egypt and the last cataract of the Nile had hitherto been considered the utmost verge of civilization and science. More distant regions were now explored. The more early travellers Bruce and his forerunners first led the way by crossing the Nubian desert, others soon followed who penetrated up the Nile, keeping near its banks, where they discovered that succession of monuments which has excited so much astonishment among all lovers of antiquity as well by their numbers as their magnitude. Temple after temple appeared, sometimes erected upon, at others excavated in the rocks and the earth; scarcely had the traveller left one than another arose to his view. Colossal figures buried up to their shoulders in sand still towered above all these which lay concealed behind them. As the travellers continued their journey an immense number of pyramids appeared with temples and ruins of cities close by or intermingled with them and at last the distant Meroë itself and the ancient temple of Jupiter Ammon still erect and majestic in its ruins.

The valley of the Nile was once covered on both sides with villages of which Pliny has left us the names and only the names of twenty on each side; in his time they no longer existed and he informs us that they were not destroyed by Roman wars, but by the earlier contentions between Ethiopia and Egypt. (Heeren).

Meroë is of special interest as the royal city of Ethiopia. Here the Ethiopian or Negro kings and princes first saw the light of day and among them and their subjects the first seeds of civilization took root. All the early royal personages of which we have any record resided at Meroë. In the eighth century, B. C. Napata was the capital — "a city of great wealth, filled with costly stone temples, avenues of sphinxes adorned the approaches to these sacred edifices.

This is the period in which the three mighty conquerors, Sabaco, Sevechus and Tirharkah directed their weapons against Egypt.

COMMERCE OF MEROË.

Ethiopians. II.

"As one passes beyond the land of the midday the Ethiopian land is that which extends furthest of all lands towards the sunset. This produces gold in abundance and large elephants and trees of all kinds growing wild and ebony and men who of all men are the tallest the most beautiful and *the most long lived.*" (Herodotus.)

The Ethiopians were the most noted people of early antiquity. ("They were a civilized people who dwelt in cities, who erected temples and other edifices, who, though without letters, had hieroglyphics, who had government and laws and the fame of whose progress in knowledge and the social arts spread in the earliest ages over a considerable part of the earth.") From the remotest times to the present one of the most celebrated yet mysterious of nations. In the earliest traditions of all the more civilized nations of antiquity the name of this distant people is found. The annals of the Egyptian priests were full of them; the nations of inner Asia on the Euphrates and Tigris have interwoven the fictions of the Ethiopians with their own traditions of the conquests and wars of their heroes, and at a period equally remote they glimmer in Greek mythology. When the Greeks scarcely knew Italy and Sicily by name the Ethiopians were celebrated in the verses of their poets. "They are the remotest nation, the most just of men, the favorites of the gods. The lofty inhabitants of Olympus journey to them and take part in their feasts. Their sacrifices are the most agreeable of all that mortals can offer them" and when the faint gleam of tradition gives way to the clear light of history, the lustre of the Ethiopian is not diminished. They still continue the object of curiosity and admiration, and the pen of cautious clear sighted historians often places them in the highest rank of knowledge and civilization.[1]

In Scripture they occupy a prominent place. Zipporah, the wife of Moses, the illustrious lawgiver, was an Ethiopian and prior to his flight into Midian Moses married Tharbis, an Ethiopian princess. Queen Candace, whose eunuch Phillip baptized, was an Ethiopian and not the only Ethiopian queen by that name, the title being used in the same way as Pharaoh for the ruler of Egypt and Caesar for Rome. Ebed-Melech, who rescued the prophet Jeremiah from the pit prison was an Ethiopian enunch. The Ethiopian Zerah who went out to meet Asa with a host of a thousand thous-

[1] Heeren p. 290.

and men and three hundred chariots was so formidable a general that special divine favor alone saved Asa from inglorious defeat. Solomon's renowned visitor, Makeda, queen of Sheba, was an Ethiopian sovereign. Tirharkah, the mere rumor of whose coming caused Sennacherib and his army to flee from their already fortified positions was one of the greatest Ethiopian conquerors and rulers of antiquity, second only to his father, Piankhi, the Negro Pharaoh who subdued all Egypt and whose reign was the beginning of Ethiopian supremacy. The foregoing is but a hint of the Negro's illustrious ancestry upon which modern research is shedding new light every day. He not only bore the cross but wore a crown. All true Christians are cross-bearers in a religious sense but it does not necessarily follow that we must be burden bearers for our brethren — such a theory belongs to the pessimist. To bear the cross of Christ is a signal honor and privilege which could in nowise bring misery to a people. We have confounded the crosses placed upon us by our more fortunate brethren with that borne by Simon the Cyrenian. We have thus submitted uncomplainingly to an unnatural burden.

This view, however, has been ably sustained by many learned men notably among them Prof. Heeren, whose inferences seem most logical and whom we shall quote at length.

Commerce of Meroë.

In proportion as we ascend into the primeval ages, the closer seems the connection between Egypt and Ethiopia. The Hebrew poets seldom mention the former without the latter; the inhabitants of both are drawn as commercial nations. When Isaiah, or rather a later poet in his name, celebrates the victories of Cyrus, their submission is spoken of as his most magnificent reward. "The trade of the Egyptians and the merchandise of the Ethiopians, and of the tall men of Saba will come over to thee and become thine own." When Jeremiah extols the great victory of Nebuchadnezzar over Pharaoh Neco near Carchemish, the Ethiopians are allied to the Egyptians. When Ezekiel threatens the downfall of Egypt, the remotest parts of Ethiopia tremble at the denunciation.

Every page indeed of Egyptian history exhibits proofs of the close intimacy in which they stood. The primitive states of Egypt . . . . derived their origin from these remote regions.

Thebes and Meroë founded in common a colony in Libya. Ethiopian conquerors more than once invaded Egypt. Egyptian kings in return forced their way into Ethiopia, the same worship, the same manners and customs, the same mode of writing are found in both countries; and under Psammatichus the noble and numerous party of malcontents retired into Ethiopia. Does not this intimate connection presuppose a permanent alliance which could only have been formed and maintained by a long peacable and friendly intercourse?

Egypt also, as far as history reaches back, abounded in all the commodities of the southern regions. Whence did she obtain the spices and drugs with which so many thousand of her dead were embalmed? Whence the incense which burned on her altars? Whence that immense quantity of cotton in which her inhabitants were clad and which her own soil produced so sparingly?

Further, whence came into Egypt that early rumor of the Ethiopian gold countries, which Cambyses set out to discover and lost half his army in the attempt? Whence that profusion of ivory and ebony with which the ancient artists of Greece and Palestine embellished? Whence that general and early spread of the name of Ethiopia which glimmers in the traditional history of so many nations, and which is celebrated as well by the Jewish poets as the earliest Grecian bards? Whence all this if the deserts which surrounded that people had formed an impassible barrier between them and the inhabitants of the northern district? Yet why should I invoke the traditions that have so long slept? Let the remains of those proud monuments which extend in one unbroken line from Elephantis and Philae beyond the desert to Meroë now speak for themselves. However short and monosyllabic their language, they plainly evince that close connection must have prevailed between the two nations that erected them, a connection between the richest and most productive regions of the earth; the gold countries of eastern Africa, the spice regions of India and the native land of frankincense, precious stones and drugs in Southern Arabia.

The Relation in Which Commerce Stood in These Regions with Religion.

Commerce and religion have always been indissolubly connected in the East. All trade and commercial intercourse requires peaceable and secure places in which it may be transacted. In the limited countries of Europe inhabited by nations partly or altogether civilized every city, indeed almost every hamlet affords this. How totally different is the case in the immeasurable tracts of the East? The rich caravans here have often to perform journeys of hundreds of miles through nations of nomad robbers. The mart is not where they might choose, but on the boundaries of the desert, where nature herself fixes it in the midst or in the neighborhood of these roving hordes. What can protect commerce here but the sanctity of the place? Where are their asylums except under the walls of the temple?

Besides, a profitable and ready sale of merchandise requires resorting together of men; and where does this take place so frequently and to such an extent as in the vicinity of the national sanctuaries, where whole nations celebrate their feasts. Here where men give themselves up to good living; the necessaries of life will be plentiful, and here the merchant will obtain the best profits. Now, however, the East affords a striking example of the extent to which the trade by sea has diminished that by land. Mecca remains still through its holy sanctuary the chief mart for the commerce of Arabia and what are the great caravans of pilgrims which journey thither from Asia and Africa but trading caravans? Are not the fairs which depend upon them the greatest in Asia?

The rapidity with which a place rises in the East, when once it has obtained a sanctuary that becomes the object of pilgrimage and by that means becomes a place of trade, almost surpasses belief. Tenta, a city of the Delta, is celebrated as containing the sepulchre of a Mohammetan Mohomitan saint Seyd Achmed. The veneration in which this is held brings an incredible number of pilgrims, who come at the time of the spring equinox and summer solstice, from Egypt, Abysinnia, Arabia and Darfour. Their number is stated at one hundred and fifty thousand.

The whole organization of social life in these parts contributes towards it.

These periodical assemblies, besides the worship of the saint, are devoted to commerce; and each of them is a period of a celebrated fair which lasts for many days and at which the produce of Upper Egypt, the coast of Barbary and the whole of the East is exchanged for the cattle of the Delta and the linen there manufactured.

The fame of the Ethiopians as a civilized people had forced its way into Greece in the time of Homer and referred preeminently to Meroë. The hundred gated Thebes is celebrated by the same poet. The traditions of Jupiter Ammon in Libya are interwoven with most ancient Greek Mythi (Dioatorus 1, p. 237) and that the Carthaginian coasts was a theatre of these mythi is generally known from the Argonautic expedition, the Triton sea, the garden of the Hesperides, the Gorgons, etc.

All this proves that rumors of these regions and places travelled very early into the West; and is it not evident that these should be understood of the places, which were the seats of national commerce?

The chief places of this trade were likewise establishments of the priest caste who as a dominant race had their principal seat at Meroë whence they sent out colonies which in their turn became builders of cities and temples and likewise the founders of states.

No doubt therefore can exist respecting the close connection between trade and religion here, nor respecting the manner in which more than one state can be formed in the interior of Africa in very high antiquity.

Notwithstanding the part which nomads took in conducting it, the trade itself still remained in the hands of Meroë and Auxum, who carried it on by their *foreign settlements* and these places still remain what nature herself has appointed, the great marts for the southern commerce.

Thus the great conclusion so interesting and important for human nature and its history, becomes in a manner forced upon us; the first seats of commerce were also the first seats of civilization; exchange of merchandise led to exchange of ideas and by this mutual friction was first kindled the sacred flame of moral and intellectual culture.

That this civilization of the Ethiopians, that is, of the ruling priest caste, was bound to their religion is easily shown. Some scientific knowledge must indisputably have been connected with it else the erection of these monuments would have been impossible.

Diodorus derives the civilization of the Egyptians in general from Ethiopia. Champollion by comparing the manners and customs, the political institutions and physical organizations of the Egyptians with those of other nations regards it as certain that they are a genuine African descended race.

The Ethiopians possessed the art of writing, not however, alphabetical characters but merely picture writing, a proof of which is still preserved upon the ruins of Meroë and from this passage the first invention of it has been attributed to them. The invention of this kind of writing would be nowhere more easy than among a people with so decided a bias for the pictorial arts nor the use and perfectioning of it more natural than in a state whose government, next to religion, was founded upon trade. A very interesting fact, however, is recorded by Diodorus; namely that the knowledge of picture writing in Ethiopia was not a privilege confined solely to the caste of priests as in Egypt, but that every one might attain it as freely as they might in Egypt the writing in common use. This, then, is a powerful proof of its being applied to the purposes of trade. A great commercial nation altogether without writing surely could never exist. Hieroglyphics were quite adequate for the caravan trade whose regular course and simple merchandise demanded but few accounts.

The fame of the piety and justice of the Ethiopians, true even to our day among African natives, spread to the most distant regions even to the Greeks. They are the first virtues which would be cultivated in a nation whose government was established by religion and commerce and not by violence and oppression.

The progress this nation had made in the pictorial arts is still one of the greatest problems, though one of the greatest certainties. The ruins of those colossal monuments, more or less preserved, still lie there and will remain the everlasting proofs of the awful magnificence of their architecture.[1]

Walking among ruins the traveller forgets the present to contemplate the past and amid the traces of a degenerate race mark the remains of a mighty nation.

"The flourishing period of Meroë was 700–800 B. C., the period in which the three mighty conquerors, Sabaco, Sevechus and Tirharkah or Tarhaco started up as conquerors and directed their weapons against Egypt, to which at least Upper Egypt became an easy prey, the unfortunate troubles of the dodecarchy having just taken place. According to Eusibius, Sabaco reigned twelve,

[1] A. H. L. Hieren: Extracts from Com. of Meroë.

Sevechus twelve and Tirharkah twenty years. Herodotus mentions only Sabaco, to whom he gives a reign of fifty years, which covers the whole dynasty." Later research, however, has given us five Ethiopian kings of pure stock: Piankhi, Shabaka, Shabataka, Tirharkah and Tamitamon, all of whose reigns we have been able to give in detail under Mr. Breasted's "Ethiopian Supremacy."

Herodotus gives an interesting account of the reign of Sabaco the Ethiopian. He was a just king, who punished crime not by putting to death, but passed sentence according to the magnitude of the offence, that imposed being to throw up mounds or dams about the city to which they belonged, thus making the cities higher.

After a reign of fifty years, remembering that the oracle had said he was to remain in Egypt for that length of time and having had a vision that seemed to bode ill, he returned to Ethiopia. This shows their great faith in and dependence upon the oracle of Ammon.

Sevechus was the contemporary of Hosea, king of Israel, whose reign ended 722, and of Salmanasar.

Tirharkah was the contemporary of his successor, Sennacherib, and deterred him in the year 714 B. C. from the invasions of Egypt merely by the rumor of his advance against him. His name was not unknown to the Greeks. Eratosthenes, in Strabo, mentions him as a conqueror who had penetrated into Europe and as far as the pillars of Hercules, that is, as a great conqueror. Meroë must have ranked at this time as a very important state and we shall find this to be the case if we go back about two hundred years to the time of Asa, the great grandson of Solomon, but who nevertheless mounted the throne of Judah within twenty years after his grandsires death, 955. "Against him went out Zerah, the Ethiopian, with a host of a thousand thousand men and three hundred chariots." This is a proof of the mightiness of the empire which at this time probably comprised Arabia Felix, but the chariots of war, which were never in use in Arabia, prove that the passage refers to Ethiopia. Zerah's exhibition took place in the early part of Asa's reign, about nine hundred and fifty years before Christ, and such an empire could not be quite a new one. We are led by undoubted historical statements up to the period of Solomon, about 1000 B. C. Further back than this the annals of history are silent but the monuments now begin to speak and confirm that high antiquity which general opinion and the tradition of Meroë attribute to this state. The name of Rameses or Sesostris has been found upon many of the Nubian monuments, and that he was the conqueror of Ethiopia is known from history. The period in which he flourished cannot be placed later than fifteen hundred years before the Christian era. But the name of Thutmosis, belonging to the preceding dynasty, has also been found in Nubia, and that assuredly upon one of the most ancient monuments of Armada. But in this sculpture, as well as in the procession representing the victory over Ethiopia, in the offering of the booty, there appears a degree of civilization which shows an acquaintance with the peaceful arts; they must consequently be attributed to a nation that had long been formed.

ETHIOPIAN SUPREMACY.

Ethiopia, sable goddess, from her ebon throne now stretches forth in royal majesty Her ebon sceptor o'er the ancient world.

"I am born of the loins created from the egg of the Diety. I have not acted without his knowledge; he ordained that I should so act." This was the declaration of Piankhi, an Ethiopian monarch of Egypt, when marching against the native princes that had revolted from him. This assertion embodies the pride of birth that characterized the Ethiopian of antiquity. They knew that they were a great people and under a special dispensation. They believed that they had a covenant with the Diety, and all the privileges and obligations that went with it, all this favor having come to them through their merits of good principle and acceptable conduct.

Lower Nubia had been dominated by the Egyptians for over eighteen hundred years while the country above the second cataract to the region of the fourth cataract had for the most part been under Egyptian control for something like a thousand years. The fertile and productive land below the fourth cataract, the rich gold mines in the mountains east of Lower Nubia, which compensated in some measure for its agricultural poverty, and the active trade from the Sudan which was constantly passing through the country made it a land of resources and possibilities which the Egyptianized Nubian, slowly awakening to his birthright, was now beginning to realize.

"Sheshouk I. had still held Nubia and it is probable that the cataract country was still a dependency of Egypt until the middle of the Twenty-second Dynasty, about 850 B. C. Nubia had for five centuries been very closely connected with Thebes and the temple of Amon. The control of the Theban High Priest had finally strengthened into full possession of Nubia for two hundred and fifty years. It must have been the Theban priesthood, perhaps as political exiles, who founded the Amonite theocracy which now as a fully developed Nubian king emerges upon our view, with its seat of government at Napata, just below the fourth cataract. Napata had been an Egyptian frontier station from the days of Amenhotep II. seven hundred years earlier. It was the remotest point in Egyptian Nubia and hence safest from attack from the north."

The state which arose here was in accordance with our explanation of its origin, a reproduction of the Amonite theocracy at Thebes.

The state god was Amon and he continually intervened directly in the affairs of government by specific oracles. The king bore all the Pharaonic titles, calling himself Lord of the Two Lands as if he governed all Egypt. He built temples of Egyptian architecture, decorated with Egyptian reliefs and bearing hieroglyphic inscriptions and dedications of the traditional Egyptian form. By 721 B. C. we suddenly find Pianki, the Nubian (Negro) king, then over twenty years upon the throne, in possession of Upper Egypt as far north as Heracleopolis just south of the Fayum, with Nubian * (Negro) garrisons in the more important towns. At this time the Twenty-third Dynasty, represented by Osorkon III at Bubastis, was no longer actually ruling more than the district of Bubastis and surrounded by rivals in every important town in the Delta. This

* Nubian here we interpret as Negro.

Saite had subdued all his neighbors in the western Delta and, beginning the absorption of Upper Egypt, had already captured Hermopolis. Painkhi sent an army against him which drove him back into the Delta and began the siege of Hermopolis. Several months later Piankhi himself reached Hermopolis with reinforcements and vigorously pushed the siege, soon forcing the surrender of the place.

The advance to the Delta, sailing down the Bahr Yusuf, was then begun, and the chief towns of the west side surrendered one after another on seeing Piankhi's force. The Nubian (Negro) king offered sacrifice to the gods in all the cities which he passed and took possession of all the available property for his own treasury and the estate of Amon. On reaching Memphis it was found to be very strongly fortified by Tefnakhte who exhorted the garrison to rely on their strong walls, their plentiful supplies and the high water which protected the east side from attack, while he rode away northward for reinforcements. Having landed on the north of the city, Piankhi, surprised at the strength of the place, devised a shrewd plan of assault, which speaks highly for his skill as a strategist. The high walls on the west of the city had been recently raised still higher, and it was evident that the east side, protected by waters, perhaps artificially raised, was being neglected.

Here was the harbour, where the ships now floated so high that their bow ropes were fastened among the houses of the city. Piankhi sent his fleet against the harbour and quickly captured all the shipping. Then taking command in person he rapidly ranged the captured craft, together with his own fleet, along the eastern walls, thus furnishing footing for his assaulting lines which he immediately sent over the ramparts and captured the city, before its eastern defenses could be strengthened against him.

The entire region of Memphis then submitted, whereupon the Delta dynasts also appeared in numbers with gifts for Piankhi and signified their submission. Piankhi now crossed the river and followed the old sacred road to Heliopolis, where he camped by the harbour. His annals narrate at length how he entered the holy of holies of the sun-god here, that he might be recognized as his son and heir to the throne of Egypt, according to the custom since the remote days of the Fifth Dynasty. Here King Osorkon III of the Twenty-third Dynasty at Bubastis, now but a petty dynast like the rest, visited Piankhi and recognized the Nubian's suzerainty. Having then moved his camp to a point just east of Athribis, Piankhi there received the submission of the principal Delta bards, fifteen in number.

Meantime the desperate Tefnakhte, having been driven from his last fortress, had taken refuge on one of the remote islands in the western mouths of the Nile. Many miles of vast Delta morass and network of irrigation canals separated Piankhi from the fugitive.

It would have been a hazardous undertaking to dispatch an army into such a region. When therefore, Tefnakhte sent gifts and an humble message of submission requesting that Piankhi send to him a messenger with whom he might go to a neighboring temple and take the oath of allegiance to his Nubian suzerian, Piankhi was very glad to accept the proposal. This done, a Nubian Pharaoh had obtained complete recognition, had supplanted the Libyans and was lord of all Egypt.

When his Delta vassals had paid Piankhi a last visit,

he loaded his ships with the riches of the North and sailed away to his southern capital amid the acclamation of the people. Arrived at Napata, Piankhi erected in the temple of Amon a magnificent granite stela, inscribed on all four sides, recording in detail the entire campaign. It is the clearest and most rational account of a military expedition which has survived from ancient Egypt.

It is this document of course which has enabled us to follow Piankhi in his conquest of the North (Bar. IV, 796–883). Tefnakhte, while he had nominally submitted to Piankhi, only awaited the withdrawal of the Ethioian to resume his designs. He eventually succeeded in establishing a kingdom of Lower Egypt, assumed the Pharaonic titles and ruled at least eight years over a feudal state like that of the Twenty-second Dynasty. His reign is parallel with the last years of the Twenty-third Dynasty, which seems to have struggled on at Bubastis as vassal princes under him. In Upper Egypt Pankhi controlled Thebes long enough to do some slight building in the temple of Mut.

In order to gain the control of the fortune of Amon with an appearance of legitimacy, Piankhi had caused his sister-wife, Amenardis, to be adopted by Shepnupet, the daughter of Osorkon III, who was sacerdotal princess of Thebes. The device was probably not new. But as Piankhi withdrew, the decadent Twenty-third Dynasty put forth its last expiring effort and established an ephemeral authority in Thebes. Piankhi's invasion of Egypt and entire reign there seems therefore to have fallen into the reign of Osorkon III.

But the rising power of Sais soon overwhelmed the failing Bubastites and Bocchoris son of Tefnakhte of Sais, gained the throne of Lower Egypt about 718 B. C., to be later known as the founder and, in so far as we know, the sole king of the Twenty-fourth Dynasty.

Egypt had now been under the divided authority of numerous local dynasts for probably over a century and a half. With its vast works of irrigation slowly going to ruin, its roads unprotected, intercourse between cities unsafe, and the large communities suffering from constant turmoil and agitation, the productive capacity of the country was steadily waning, while foreign commerce disappeared. The hopeless state of the country was clearly understood by the sagacious Isaiah, who declared to his people "Behold the Lord rideth upon a swift cloud and cometh unto Egypt; and the idols of Egypt shall be moved at his presence, and the heart of Egypt shall melt in the midst of it. And I will stir up the Egyptians against the Egyptians; and they shall fight every one against his brother and every one against his neighbor; city against city and kingdom against kingdom. And I will give over the Egyptians into the hand of a cruel lord, and a fierce king shall rule over them saith the Lord the Lord of Hosts. The princes of Zoan are utterly foolish the counsel of the wisest counsellors of Pharaoh is become brutish.

The princes of Zoan are become fools; the princes of Noph (Napata) are deceived; they have caused Egypt to go astray that are the cornerstone of her tribes. The Lord hath mingled a spirit of perverseness in the midst of her. They have caused Egypt to go astray in every work thereof as a drunken man staggering in his vomit. Neither shall there be for Egypt any work which head or tail, palm branch or rush, may do." (Is. XIX.) No truer picture could possibly be portrayed.

SHABAKA (REIGN OF).

Some ten years after the retirement of Piankhi, the Nubian kings again appeared in the North. Piankhi had now been succeeded by his brother Shabaka, with whom the uninterrupted series of pure Ethiopian royal names begins. We possess no native records of his conquest of the country, but Manetho states that he burned Bocchoris alive. Lower Egypt was subdued, Ethiopian Supremacy acknowledged, and Shabaka entrenched himself so firmly that he became founder of the Twenty-fifth Dynasty (or Ethiopian) as reported by Manetho. Appreciating the serious danger of Assyria's presence on his very borders, Shabaka immediately sent his agents among the Syro-Palestinian states to excite them to revolt. In Philistia, Judah, Moabaud, Edom, he promised the vassals of Assyria support in rebellion against their Ninevite Suzerain.

Remembering the ancient supremacy of Egypt, failing to understand the state of decadent importance into which she had fallen, and anxious to shake off oppressive Assyrian yoke, they lent a ready ear to the emissaries of Shabaka. Only in Judah did the prophet statesman, Isaiah, foresee the futility of depending upon Egypt, and the final catastrophe which should overtake her at the hands of Assyria. The vigilant Assyrian, however, hearing of the projected alliance, acted so quickly that the conspirators were glad to drop their designs and protest fidelity. In spite of difficulties in Babylon and rebellions in the north, the able and aggressive Sargon pushed the consolidation of his power with brilliant success and left to his son Sennacherib in 705 B. C. the first stable and firmly compacted empire ever founded by a Semitic power.[1]

[1] Is. XX. Wang: Bar IV, 920.

Sennacherib was embarrassed in his earlier years with the usual complications in Babylon. Maraduk-baliddin (Mero-dach-Baladan) an able and active claimant of the Babylonian throne, who had already caused Sennacherib's father much trouble, now sent his emissaries to stir up defection and create a diversion in his favor in the west. As a result Luli, the energetic king of Tyre, Hezekiah of Judah, the dynasts of Edom, Moab and Ammon with the chiefs of their Beduin neighbors, in fact all the southern half of the Assyrian conquests in the west besides Egypt, were finally organized in a great alliance against Nineveh. Before the allies could act in concert Sennacherib suddenly appeared in the west, marched down the Phoenician coast, capturing all its strongholds save Tyre; and pressed on southward to the revolting Philistine cities. Here having punished Askalon he advanced to Altaqu, where he came upon the mother army gathered by the tardy Shabaka among his northern vassals whom Sennacherib calls "the Kings of Mucri (Egypt).

We know nothing of the strength of this force, although Sennacherib claims that they were "without number"; but it is safe to conclude that it was not a formidable army. A loose aggregation of levies from the domains of the local Delta princes was little fitted to meet the compact and finely organized armies which the Assyrian kings had gradually developed till they had become the dread and terror of the west. Although small Egyptian contingents had before served as auxiliaries against the Assyrians, the armies of the two empires on the Nile and the Tigris had never before faced each other. Sennacherib led his own power in person while the Egyptian army was entrusted by Shabaka to his nephew, a son of Piankhi named Taharka (Tirharkah), who some thirteen or fourteen years afterward became king of Ethiopia — a fact which led the Hebrew annalist to give him that title already at the time of this campaign. There was but one possible issue for the battle; Sennacherib disposed of Taharka's army without difficulty; having meanwhile beleagered Jerusalem, the plague infected winds from the malarial shores east of the Delta had scattered death among his troops. This overwhelming catastrophe, together with disquieting news from Babylon, forced him hastily to retire to Nineveh, thus bringing to Jerusalem the deliverance promised by Isaiah, an event in which pious tradition afterwards saw the destroying angel of the Lord. This deliverance was perhaps as fortunate for Egypt as Jerusalem. For the third time the invincible Assyrian army had stood on the very threshold of Egypt and still the decrepit nation on the Nile was spared the inevitable humiliation which was now so near. The Syro-Palestinian princes, however, were so thoroughly cowed that Egypt was thenceforth unable to seduce them to rebellion. Like the Hebrews, they at last recognized the truth, as mockingly stated by the officers of Sennacherib to the unhappy ambassadors of Jerusalem; "Now behold, thou trusted upon the staff of this bruised reed, even upon Egypt; whereon if a man lean it will go into his hand and pierce it; so is Pharaoh king of Egypt unto all that trust on him."[1]

Shabaka apparently ruled his vassal Egyptian states for the remainder of his reign in peace. The fragments of a clay tablet bearing the seal of Shabaka and a king

[1] Kings II. XIX.

of Assyria, found at Kuyunjek may indicate some agreement between the two nations. At Thebes, Shabaka reinstated his sister, Amenardis, who must have been temporarily expelled by Osorkon III.

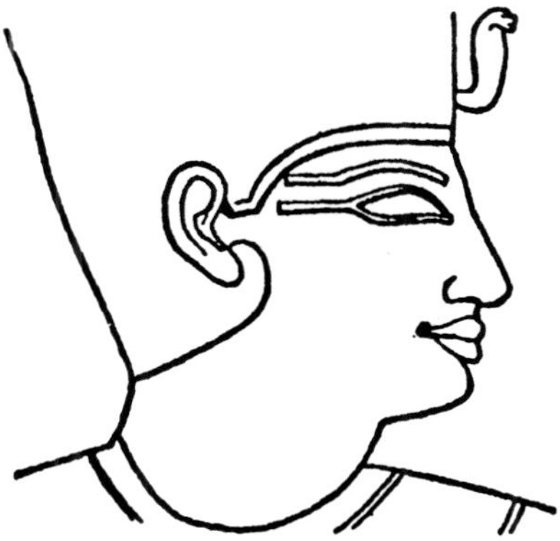

SHABAK-*Sabaco.*

He built a chapel at Karnak and his building operations necessitated an expedition to the distant quarries of Hammamat. We also find records of his temple restorations at Thebes and it is evident that he governed Egypt at least in his relations with the temples, precisely as a native Pharaoh would have done. It was probably Shabaka who now broke the power of the High Priest at Amon, of whose importance we shall see further as we proceed.

SHABATAKA.

About 700 B. C. Shabaka was succeeded by Shabataka another Ethiopian whose connection with the reigning Ethiopian or Nubian family is a little uncertain, although Manetho, who calls him Sebichos, makes him a son of

Shabaka. As the western vassals remained quiet and Sennacherib was now absorbed in his operations at the other extremity of his empire, Shabataka was unmolested by the Assyrian.

SHABATOK-*Sevechus.*

His name is rare in Egypt but it is evident from the conditions which survived him that he was entirely unable to exterminate the local dynasts and consolidate the power of Egypt. His reign ended about 688 B. C.

TAHARKA (TIRHARKAH).

It is at this juncture that we can trace the rising fortunes of a son of Piankhi, prince Taharka, whose features as preserved in contemporary sculptures show unmistakable negroid characteristics. He had been entrusted with the command of the army in the campaign against Sennacherib. While we know nothing of the circumstances which brought about his advent to the throne, Manetho states that leading an army from

Ethiopia he slew Sebichos, who must be Shabataka, and seized the crown. The contemporary monuments, without intimation of these events, abruptly picture him in Tanis as king, summoning his mother, whom he has not seen in many years, from Napata to Tanis, that she may assume her proper station as queen mother there. In view of this fact and the trouble to be anticipated from Assyria, it is not improbable that the Ethiopians at this time maintained Tanis as their Egyptian residence.

TAHRAKA-*Tirhaka.*

For some thirteen years Taharka ruled his kingdom without interference from Assyria. The west had for twenty years seen nothing of Sennacherib, who was now assassinated by his son in 681 B. C. As soon as Esarhaddon could arrange the affairs of the great empire to which he had succeeded, he determined to resort to the only possible remedy for the constant interference of Egypt with the authority of Assyria in Palestine, viz., the conquest of the Nile country and humiliation of the Pharaoh. With farseeing thoroughness he laid his plans for the execution of this purpose and his army was knocking at the frontier fortresses of the eastern Delta in 674 B. C. But Taharka, who was a man of far greater ability than his two Ethiopian predecessors, must have made a supreme effort to meet the crisis. The outcome of the battle (673 B. C.) was unfavorable for the Assyrian, if indeed, as the documents perhaps indicate, the Assyrian did not suffer positive defeat. But Esarhaddon nevertheless quietly continued his preparations for the conquest of Egypt. Baal, king of Tyre, perhaps encouraged by the indecisive result of the first Assyrian invasion, then rebelled, making common cause with Taharka. In 670 B. C. Esarhaddon was again in the west at the head of his forces. Having invested Tyre, he defeated and scattered the Egyptian army. As the Ethiopian fell back upon Memphis Esarhaddon pressed him closely and beseiged and captured the city, which fell a rich prey to the cruel and rapacious Ninevite army. Fleeing southward, Taharka abandoned Lower Egypt, which was immediately organized by Esarhaddon into dependencies of Assyria.

He records the names of twenty lords of the Delta formerly Ethiopian vassals who now took the oath of fealty to him. Among these names, written in cuniform, a number may be recognized as those of the same men with eighteen of whom Piankhi had to deal in the same region.

Necho, doubtless descendant of Tefnakhte occupies the most prominent place among them as prince of Sais and Memphis. The list also includes a prince of Thebes, but Esarhaddon possessed no more than a nominal authority in Upper Egypt at this time. As he returned to Nineveh northward along the coast road he hewed in the rock at the Dog River, beside the triumphant stelar of Rameses II, a record of his great achievement, while in Samal in North Syria he erected a similar monument representing himself, of heroic stature, leading two captives, of whom one is probably Baal of Tyre and the other, as his negroid features indicate, is the unfortunate Taharka.

After the domination of Libyan and Nubian in turn, Egypt was now a prey to a third foreign conqueror who, however, differed essentially from the others in that he resided abroad and evinced not the slightest sympathy with Egyptian institutions and customs. The result was that the Delta kinglets who had sworn allegiance to the Ninevite immediately plotted with Taharka for the resumption of his rule in Lower Egypt, which he thereupon assumed without much delay on the withdrawal of the Assyrian army. Esarhaddon was thus forced to begin his work over again; but in 668 B. C., while on the march to resume operations in Egypt, he died. With but slight delay his son Ashurbanipal continued the campaign, and placed one of his commanders in charge of the expedition.

Between Memphis and the frontier, eastern Delta Taharka was again routed. He fled to Thebes this time pursued by the Assyrians who made the forty days march thither determined to expel him from Egypt. Whether the enemy actually captured Thebes at this time is somewhat doubtful. In any case Ashurbanipal was unable to extend his authority to Upper Egypt. He had hardly restored his supremacy in the Delta when his rivals there again began communicating with Taharka purposing his restoration as before. But this correspondence with Taharka was discovered by the Assyrian officials in Egypt and they were sent to Nineveh in chains. There the wily Necho, whom Esarhaddou had made king of Sais, was able to win the confidence of Ashurbanipal, who pardoned him, loaded him with honors and restored him to his kingdom in Sais while his son was appointed to rule Athribis. At the same time Ashurbanipal accompanied him with Assyrian officials intended, of course, to be a check upon his conduct. Taharka was now unable to gain any further foothold among the Assyrian vassals in the Delta. He probably held Thebes, where he controlled the fortune of Amon by causing his sister Shepnupet to be adopted by Amenardis the "Divine Votress or sacerdotal princess of Thebes, who had been appointed by Piankhi in the same way. At Napata, Taharka built two considerable temples and the Ethiopian capital evidently became a worthy royal residence in his time.

He was an enterprising prince engaged in many wars and a determined opponent of the Assyrian. His name is read on Egyptian monuments as Tahark or Torek and his face which appears on them is expressive of determination. In the latter part of his life, his star ultimately paled but not from any lack of courage or resolution or good faith on his part. He struggled gallantly against the Assyrian power for above thirty years, was never wanting to his confederates and was among the most distinguished monarchs of his race and period.

(Note). Poselleni in exploring the tomb of a nurse of a daughter of Taharka at Thebes found beside the mummy in a case of wood a bronze mirror with a cover which protected it from the air and turned aside on a pin to allow of its being used. The polished surface of the mirror retained enough of its brightness when discovered to reflect the face.

Taharka survived but a few months his appointment of Tanutamon, a son of Shabaka as co-regent, who then succeeded to the crown in 663 B. C.

Tanutamon.

Encouraged by a favorable dream Tanutamon undertook the recovery of Lower Egypt, defeated the Assyrian commander, retook Memphis and demanded the submission of the Delta dynasts. He had hardly settled in Memphis, when Ashurbanipal's army appeared and drove the Ethiopian for the last time from Lower Egypt. The Assyrians pursued him to Thebes, and as he ingloriously withdrew southward, they sacked and plundered the magnificent capital of Egypt's age of splendor.

As the Assyrians withdrew from Thebes, Tanutamon again entered the desolated city where he maintained himself for at least six years more till 655 B. C. By 654 B. C. he had disappeared from Thebes whether by death or retirement and his disappearance was the termination of Ethiopian Supremacy in Egypt.

Withdrawing to Napata the Ethiopians never made another attempt to subdue the kingdom of the Lower river but gave their attention to the development of Nubia.[1]

IV.

THE MACROBIAN ETHIOPIANS.

By Herodotus.

Cambyses planned three several expeditions, one against the Carthaginians, another against the Ammonians and a third against the Macrobian Ethiopians, who inhabit that part of Libya which lies upon the South Sea. In forming his plans, he determined to send a naval

[1] James Henry Breasted, Ancient Egyptians, Chap. XXVI.

force against the Carthaginians and against the Ammonians, a detachment of his land forces, and against the Ethiopians, spies in the first instance, who were to see the table of the sun which was said to exist among the Ethiopians and besides to explore other things, and to cover their design, they were to carry presents to the king. The table of the sun is said to be of the following description. There is a meadow in the suburbs filled with the cooked flesh of all sorts of quadrupeds, in this the several magistrates of the city, for some purpose, place the flesh at night, and in the day time whoever chooses comes and feasts on it. The inhabitants say, that the earth itself, from time to time produces these things. Such is the description given of what is called the table of the sun. When the Ichthyophagic spies came to Cambyses from Elephantine, he dispatched them to the Ethiopians, having instructed them what to say, carrying presents consisting of a purple cloak, a golden necklace, bracelets, an alabaster box of ointment and a cask of palm wine. These Ethiopians, to whom Cambyses sent, are said to be the tallest and handsomest of all men; and they say that they have customs different from those of other nations, and especially the following with regard to the regal power; for they confer the sovereignty upon the man whom they consider to be of the largest stature and to possess strength proportionable to his size.

When, therefore the Ichthyophagi arrived among this people, they gave the presents to the king, and addressed him as follows: "Cambyses, king of the Persians, desirous of becoming your friend and ally, has sent us, bidding us confer with you, and he presents you with these gifts, which are such as he himself most delights in." But the Ethiopian knowing that they came as spies spoke thus to them. "Neither has the king of Persia sent you with these presents to me because he valued my alliance; nor do you speak the truth, for you have come as spies of my kingdom; nor is he a just man; for if he were just, he would not desire any other territory than his own; nor would he reduce people into servitude who have done him no injury. However, give him this bow, and say these words to him: "The king of the Ethiopians advises the king of the Persians, when the Persians can thus easily draw a bow of this size, then to make war on the Macrobian Ethiopians with more numerous forces; but until that time, let him thank the gods, who have not inspired the sons of the Ethiopians with a desire of adding another land to their own." Having spoken thus and unstrung the bow he delivered it to the comers.

Then taking up the purple cloak he asked what it was and how made; and when the Ichthyophagi told him the truth respecting the purple and the manner of dyeing, he said that the men are deceptive, and their garments are deceptive also. Next he inquired about the necklace and bracelets and when the Ichthyophagi explained to him their use as ornaments, the king laughing and supposing them to be fetters, said that they have stronger fetters than these.

Thirdly, he inquired about the ointment; and when they told him about its composition and use, he made the same remark as he had on the cloak. But when he came to the wine, and inquired how it was made, being very much delighted with the draught, he farther asked what food the king made use of and what was the longest age to which a Persian lived. They answered that he fed on bread, describing the nature of wheat; and that the longest life of a Persian was eighty years. Upon this, the Ethiopian said that he was not at all surprised if men who fed on dung lived so few years; and they would not be able to live so many years, if they did not refresh themselves with this beverage showing the wine to the Ichthyophagi; for in this *he admitted* they were surpassed by the Persians. The Ichthyophagi inquiring in turn of the king concerning the life and diet of the Ethiopians, he said that most of them attained to a hundred and twenty years and some even exceeded that term, and that their food was boiled flesh and their drink milk. And when the spies expressed astonishment at the number of years, he led them to a fountain by washing in which they became sleek as if it had been of oil, and an odor proceeded from it as of violets. The water of this fountain, the spies said, is so weak that nothing is able to float upon it, neither wood nor such things as lighter than wood; but everything sinks to the bottom. If this water is truly such as it is said to be, it may be they are long lived by reason of the abundant use of it. Leaving this fountain he conducted them to the common prison, where all were fettered with golden chains; for among these Ethiopians brass is the most rare and precious of all metals. After having viewed the prison they next visited that which is called the table of the sun. After this they visited last of all their sepulchres which are said to be prepared from crystal in the following manner: when they have dried the body, either as the Egyptians do, or in some other way, they plaster it all over with gypsum, and paint it making it as much as possible resemble real life; they then put round it a hollow column made of crystal, which they dig up in abundance and is easily wrought. The body being in the middle of the column is plainly seen nor does it emit an unpleasant smell nor is it in any way offensive; and it is all visible as the body itself. The nearest relations keep the column in their houses for a year, offering to it the first fruits of all, and performing sacrifices; after that time they carry it out and place it somewhere near the city.

The spies having seen everything returned home; and when they had reported all that had passed, Cambyses, being greatly enraged immediately marched against the Ethiopians, without making any provision for the subsistence of his army or once considering that he was going to carry his arms to the remotest part of the world; but as a madman and not in possession of his senses, as soon as he heard the report of the Ichthyophagi, he set out on his march, ordering the Greeks, who were present to stay behind and taking with him all his land forces. When the army reached Thebes, he detached about fifty thousand men, and ordered them to reduce the Ammonians to slavery, and to burn the oracular temple of Jupiter, while he with the rest of his army, marched against the Ethiopians, but before the army had passed over a fifth part of the way all the provisions that they had were exhausted, and after the provisions, the beasts of burden were eaten, and likewise failed. Now if Cambyses, when he learned this, had altered his purpose, and had led back his army even after his first error, he would have proved himself to be a wise man; but now without any reflection, he still continued advancing. The soldiers, as long as they could gather any from the earth supported life by eating herbs; but when they reached the sands some of them had recourse to a horrid expedient, for, taking one man in ten by lot they devoured him. When Cambyses heard this, shocked at their eating one another, he abandoned his expedition against the Ethiopians, marched back and reached Thebes, after losing a great part from his army. From Thebes, he went down to Memphis, and suffered the Greeks to sail away. This ended the expedition against the Ethiopians.[1]

V.

NEGRO–EGYPTIAN PHARAOHS AMENOPHITES AND THOTMESITES NEW EMPIRE.

XVII. Theban Dynasty.

The Ethiopians and Egyptians being closely allied, it is not surprising that we find a marked Negro caste among the latter who were but another African people and between whom there was but slight physical differences. Their intermarriages so blending the types that there was no line of division between them, especially was this true of the ruling caste.

All sculptures and monuments of the earliest peoples are predominantly negroid. Royal heads four thousand years old belonging to the fourth dynasty recently unearthed are undoubtedly of Negro origin. Hence, Egyptian history is Negro history as we have abundant proof from the earliest dynasties through Egypt's age of splendor, the royal line was strongly imbued with the blood of the Negro, therefore we have chosen the name Negro-Egyptian as most fitting for the Pharaohs of the seventeenth dynasty, especially.

[1] Book III, 17–26.

Piankhi who won the title of Pharaoh by conquest was the first ruler of Egypt of pure Negro blood. He was the father of Tirhakra, mentioned in our Bible, the sound of whose name awed the great Sennacherib. These names and many others with which our readers will become familiar should be precious to us as they represent men who were our very own, bone of our bone and flesh of our flesh. What Cromwell was to the English, Napoleon to the French, these great Negro-Egyptian Pharaohs were to the African Negroes.

This period about 1700 B. C. begins with the reign of Aahmes, Amasis a native Egyptian, who is credited with the expulsion of the Hyksos with whom he warred five years. These wars concluded he turned his attention to the regions south of Egypt and led an expedition against them. At first he swept everything before him and victory seemed certain, but the Negroes were not such easy prey. A Nubian chief, Teta-an, rallied forces and went out and forced Aahmes back, retook the regions of the south and destroying the temples of the Egyptian garrisons and annihilating the Egyptian power." This was the beginning of a long struggle, lasting until the twenty-first year of the reign of Amasis who was finally victorious and took Teta-an prisoner. Much credit is due this chief and his army in their determined resistance to retain the control of their territory.

Aahnes having established Egyptian control over the country between the First and Second Cataract, gave himself to domestic affairs and began to repair the temples and other sacred edifices. His reign covered twenty-five years. He married an Ethiopian princess and conferred upon her the throne name of Nefert-ari-Aahmes, "the beautiful companion of Aahmes." Her complexion was of ebon blackness. This beautiful Cushite princess became his favorite wife and the mother of succeeding Pharoahs. She is called, "the daughter, sister, wife and mother of a king." This alliance between Aahmes and Nefert-ari was not merely a political one. "His queen was certainly regarded as an important personage. She was called "the wife of the god Ammon," and enjoyed some high post con-

Aahmes-Nofre-Ari.

nected with the worship of that god with Thebes; Aahbes commemorated her upon his monuments; during her son's reign she held for a time the reins of power; while in after ages she was venerated as "ancestress and founder of the eightieth dynasty."

Amenhotek I the son and successor of Aahmes reigned under the tutelage of his mother, continued the Ethiopian campaigns and embellished Thebes. He was first of the line of Negro-Egyptian Pharaohs. He was a mother's son of Cush, whose maternal grandsires were full blooded Negroes "of the best physical type." He associated his mother, the beautiful black queen, with himself in government. On his monuments his mother shares a place equal with his own. "She is joined with him in the worship of the gods; and she is "the lady of the two lands" as he is lord of them." Amenophis married an Egyptian lady, his son by her he named Thotmes. The reign of Thotmes I was marked as the period of Egypt's first attempt to carry arms into Asia and thus retaliate against the oppression she suffered from the Hyksos which resulted in a spirit of military activity and conquest covering three centuries and raised it to its zenith. Thothmes I not only extended his dominions in the south but led successive campaigns into Asia. On his return to Egypt he proceeded to enlarge and embel-

AAHMES.

THOTMES I.

lish the temple of Ammon at Thebes in return for the victories which this god was supposed to have made possible for him. His reign is supposed to have been twenty-one years.

Thotmes married Aahmes, thought to be his sister, by

whom he had a daughter and two sons, Hasheps or Hatasu, the sons, having the same name as their father, Thotmes II and Thotmes III and great grand children of Aahmes and Nefert-ari-Aahmes.

The reign of Thotmes II was uneventful except for an expedition against the Arabs. His sister Hatasu, being more ambitious for power and having an influence over him was permitted to share his throne and virtually directed the affairs of government. Together they made additions to the temples. Thotmes II's brief reign ended, Hasheps became sole ruler, and in every way as a king—masculine of mind, she donned male attire and

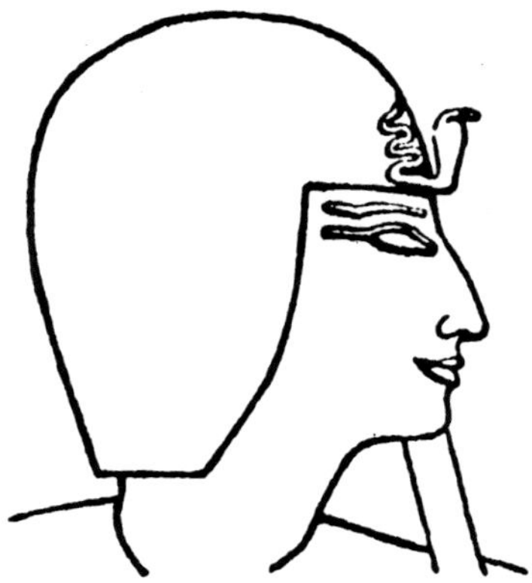

THOTMES II.

the title of a king. Her young brother was hardly more than a subject. She erected many buildings of elegant taste — obelisks at Thebes in the temple of Ammon — statues of herself in various places and extended her sovereignty over the land of Punt by means of a naval expedition which returned to Egypt laden with the wealth of the country. She tardily acknowledged the majority of her brother and reluctantly gave him recognition as sovereign by allowing his name to appear on public monuments; after having held absolute control of the government for fifteen years. A woman of wonderful executive ability, yet unscrupulous in her lust for power, her reign compared favorably with that of preceding Pharaohs. Her reign as co-regent with Thotmes III was about seven years. As great-granddaughter of the Ethiopian queen Nefert-ari-Ahames, she deserves an honored place.

THOTMES III.

Thotmes III was beyond doubt the greatest of Negro-Egyptian Pharaohs and Conquerors and has been called

THOTMES III.

"the Alexander of Egyptian history." He led an expedition into Western Asia forced the states to pay him tribute and to acknowledge his suzerainty. He carried on at least eight successive campaigns with the states of Asia covering a period from his twenty-third to his fortieth year. "Ambitious, restless, brave even to rashness, equally remarkable as a warrior and as a general successful in his naval no less than in his military operations he spread the name and fame of Egypt through distant lands alarmed the great empires of Western Asia conquered and held in subjection all Syria and Western Mesopotamia as far as the Khabour River, probably reduced Cyprus, chastised the Arabs, crushed rebellion in Nubia, and left to his successor a dominion extending above eleven hundred miles from north to south, and (in places) four hundred and fifty miles from west to east. At the same time he distinguished himself as a builder. Restorer or founder of a score of temples, designer of the great "Hall of Pillars" at Thebes, by far the largest apartment that the world has as yet seen, erector of numerous gigantic obelisks, constructor and adorner of vast propylaea, author or restorer of at least five huge colossi, he has left the impress of his presence in Egypt more widely than almost any other of her kings while at the same time he has supplied to the great capitals of the modern world their most striking Egyptian monuments.

Thotmes III died after a reign of fifty-four years, probably at about the age of sixty."[1]

Amenophis II.

Amenophis II son of Thotmes III, succeeded his father on the throne and found it necessary to put down rebellion in the states of Asia who, as was common at that period, renounced their allegiance to Egypt upon the

[1] Rawlinson's Ancient Egypt, p. 259–260.

death of Thotmes and assumed their independence. Amenophis is said to have re-established Egyptian power in all the countries previously subdued by his father, this alone was no small task and must have kept him busily employed. His architecture is said to be far inferior to that of his predecessors. His reign was of short duration. His son who succeeded him on the

Thotmes IV.

Amenoph II.

throne took the name of Thotmes that of his grandfather and was known as Thotmes IV. He was not the eldest son of Amenophis but was his father's immediate successor which he attributed to some special favor of the god Hanuachis, this god having appeared to him in a dream. In some way associating Hanuachis with the sphinx, he dug away the accumulation of sand at its base, "set up between the fore paws of the Sphinx a massive memorial tablet twelve feet high and eight feet broad on which he recorded the circumstances of his dream. In front of his memorial tablet and also within the paws of the monstrous animal he Thotmes constructed a small temple for the worship of the god with whom he identified it. One expedition against the Hittites of Syria and another against the Cushites or people of Ethiopia are all that can be assigned to him. The former he commemorated in the great temple of Ammon at Thebes, the latter in the Nubian temple of Amada."

He was a great sportsman, his favorite game was the lion hunt, a fondness for swift horses that "outstripped the wind" according to his own statement.[1]

Amenophis III.

Thotmes IV married a foreigner, an Ethiopian or Cushite, named Maut-Hemwa by whom he had a son, Amen-hotep or Amenophis who succeeded him. Amenophis III married a foreigner, Taia who was an Ethiopian. Amenophis was deeply attached to his mother, Queen Maut-Hemwa and later to his wife, Queen Taia whose advice and counsel he sought and acted upon. He gave little attention to military enterprise, the boundaries of Egypt remained the same as when he inherited the throne but his building activities more than made up the deficit. He began in the first year of his reign to excavate stone for the repair of temples and throughout his reign of thirty six years, his zeal seemed untiring in the erection of magnificent buildings which have been of greater attraction to travellers than those of any other Pharaoh. Amenophis erected the great temple of Ammon at Luxor, one of the most magnificent in all Egypt, embellished that of Karnak with a new propylon, built two new temples to Ammon and Maut and united

[1] Rawlinson's anc. Egypt Vol. II.

the whole quarter of the temples at Karnak with the new temple of Ammon at Luxor by an avenue of criosphinxes with the sun's disk on their heads (there was a leaning to this worship by Amenophis). He also built two temples to Knephor Khnum (gods) at Elephantine,

Amunoph III. Memnon.

Maut-Henwa.

one to contain his own image at Soleb in Nubia, a shrine with a propylon and ram-sphinxes before it at Gebel Berkal or Napata and another shrine at Sedinga. Inscribed tablets dated in his reign are found at Semneh in the island of Konosso on the rocks between Philae and Asscuan, at El-Kaab at Silsilis and at Sarabit-el-Khadim in the Sinaitic peninsula. Of all his edifices that which approved itself the most highly in his own eyes was the temple or rather, perhaps, the temple-palace of Luxor. "I built on the rocky soil," he says, "a court of alabaster, of rose granite and of black stone. Also a double tower gateway did I execute, because I had undertaken to dedicate the most beautiful thing possible to my divine father" (i. e. Ammon). Statues of the gods are to be seen in it everywhere. They are carved in all their parts. A great statue was made of gold and of all kinds of beautiful precious stones. I gave directions to execute O Ammon, what pleased thee well to unite thee with thy beautiful dwelling."[1]

TAIA.

His most remarkable work was the twin colossi, two gigantic statues sitting, of the Pharaoh cut out of one solid block of stone and between 60 and 70 feet high. One has been called "vocal Memnon" because of a musical sound that issued from it at day break, supposed to have been caused by a fissure in the rock, caused perhaps by earthquake, together with the action of the sun's rays upon it.

This statue was repaired by Septimus Severus, A. D. 196.

Amenophis III was a kind and benevolent ruler, crime

[1] Rawlinson's An. Egypt, Vol. II.

was punished with justice, while loyalty was often liberally rewarded. Amenophis reigned thirty-six years. He was survived by his Queen Taia.

NOTE.—In the Theban tomb, there was an amazing collection of Negro Scenes. A Negress, apparently a princess, arrives at Thebes drawn in a plastrum by a pair of humped oxen. The driver and groom are Egyptians, perhaps eunuchs. Following her, are multitudes of Negroes bringing tribute from the Upper country and slaves — red and black, Egyptian and Negro — of both sexes. They have come to make offerings in the tomb of a "royal son of Kush," Amenoph or Amenophis, and no doubt this princess is Queen Taia.

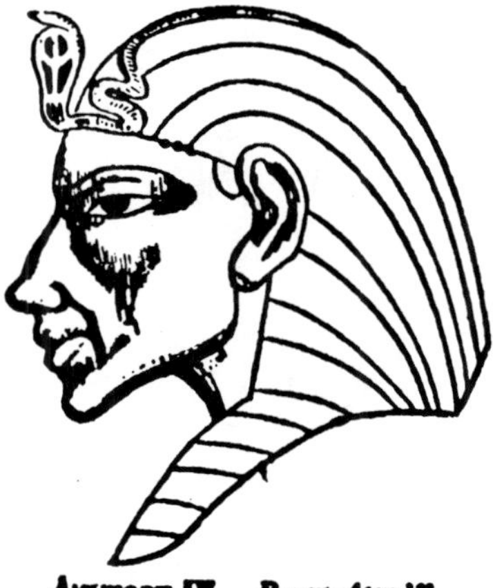

Amenoph IV. [illegible]

His son, Amenhotep IV, succeeded him to the throne. He was the founder of the "Disk Heresy," or the worship of the sun's disk. Before this new form of worship was firmly implanted the influence of the priesthood was successful in winning back to an extent, the adherents of the old form and Amenhotep found it necessary to quit Egypt. He set up an independent kingdom between Thebes and Memphis, Khu-aten, he beautified it with temples and monuments and with a large number of followers, reigned twelve years in unbroken peace. His mother was made a permanent resident of his court and enjoyed all the honors due queen mother. To his wife he was greatly devoted. "Sweet love fills my heart," he says in one inscription, "for the queen and for her young children. Grant a long life of many years to the Queen Nefert Tii; may she keep the hand of Pharaoh! Grant a long life to the royal daughter, Meri-Aten, and to the royal daughter Mak-Aten and to their children. May they keep the hand of the queen, their mother, eternally and forever. What I swear is a true avowal of what my heart says to me. Never is there falsehood in what I say."[1]

VI.

How Moses Made War with the Ethiopians.

When Moses came to the age of maturity he made his virtues manifest to the Egyptians and showed them he was born for bringing them down and raising the Israelites. And the occasion he laid hold of was this: The Ethiopians who were next neighbors to the Egyptians made an inroad into their country which they seized upon and carried off the effects of the Egyptians, who in their rage fought against them and revenged the affronts they had received from them; but being overcome in battle some of them were slain and the rest ran away in a shameful manner and by that means saved themselves whereupon the Ethiopians followed after them in the pursuit; and thinking it would be a mark of cowardice

[1] Rawlinson's An. E. Vol. II.

if they did not subdue all Egypt, they went on to subdue the rest with greater vehemence; and when they had tasted the sweets they never left of the prosecution of the war; and as the nearest parts had not courage enough, at first, to fight with them they proceeded as far as Memphis and the sea itself while not one of the cities was able to oppose them. The Egyptians under this sad oppression betook themselves to their oracles and prophecies, and when God had given them this counsel to make use of Moses, the Hebrew, and take his assistance, the king commanded his daughter to produce him, that he might be the general of the army. Upon which, when she had made him swear he would do him no harm, she delivered him to the king and supposed his assistance would be of great advantage to them. She withal, reproached the priest, who, when he had before admonished the Egyptians to kill him, was not ashamed to own their want of his help. So Moses, at the persuasion of Thermuthis and the king himself, cheerfully undertook the business; and the sacred scribes of both nations were glad, those of the Egyptians that they would once more overcome their enemies by his valor and that by the same piece of management Moses would be slain; but those of the Hebrews that they should escape from the Egyptians because Moses was to be their general.

But Moses prevented the enemies and took and led his army before those enemies were apprised of his attacking them; for he did not march by the river, but by land, where he gave a wonderful demonstration of his sagacity; for when the ground was difficult to be passed over because of the multitude of serpents, which it produces in vast numbers and indeed is singular in some of those productions which other countries do not breed and yet such as are worse than others in power and mischief and an unusual fierceness of sight, some of which ascend out of the ground unseen and also fly in the air and so come upon men at unawares, and do them a mischief, Moses invented a wonderful stratagem to preserve the army safe and without hurt; for he made baskets, like unto arks, of sedge and filled them with ibes, and carried them along with them; which animal is the greatest enemy to serpents, imaginable, for they fly from them when they come near them, and as they fly, they are caught and devoured by them as if it were done by the harts; but the ibes are tame creatures and only enemies to the serpentine kind. As soon therefore, as Moses was come to the land which was the breeder of these serpents, he let loose the ibes; and by their means repelled the serpentine kind and used them for his assistants before the army came upon the ground. When he had then proceeded thus on his journey he came upon the Ethiopians before they expected him; and joining battle with them he beat them of the hopes they had of success against the Egyptians and went on in overthrowing their cities and indeed made a great slaughter of these Ethiopians. Now when the Egyptian army had once tasted of this prosperous success, by the means of Moses, they did not slacken their diligence insomuch that the Ethiopians were in danger of being reduced to slavery and all sorts of destruction and at length they retired to Saba which was a royal city of Ethiopia and Cambyses afterward named Meroe after the name of his own sister. The place was to be beseiged with very great difficulty since it was both encompassed by the Nile, quite round and the other rivers, Asapus and Astaborus, made it a very difficult thing for such as attempted to pass over them; for the city was situated in a retired place and was inhabited after the manner of an island, being encompassed with a strong wall and having the rivers to guard from their enemies and having great ramparts between the wall and the rivers, insomuch that when the waters came with the greatest violence it can never be drowned; which ramparts make it next to impossible, for even such as are gotten over the rivers to take the city. However, while Moses was uneasy at the army's lying idle, for the enemies durst not come to battle, Tharbis, who was the daughter of the king of the Ethiopians, happened to see Moses as he led the army near to the walls; and fought with great courage, and admiring the subtility of his undertaking and believing him to be the author of the Egyptian success when they had before despaired of recovering their liberty, and to the occasion of the great danger the Ethiopians were in when they had before boasted of their great achievements, she fell deeply in love with him and upon the prevalency of that passion sent to him the most faithful of all her servants to discourse with him upon their marriage.

He thereupon accepted, the offer on condition she would procure the delivering up of the city and gave the assurance to take her to be his wife, and that when he had once taken possession of the city he would not break his oath to her. No sooner was the agreement made — it took effect immediately; and when Moses had cut off the Ethiopians, he gave thanks to God and consummated his marriage and led the Egyptians back to their own land.[1]

NOTE. The history of Moses as general of the Egyptians against the Ethiopians is wholly omitted in the Bible but is thus cited by Iraneus from Josephus and that soon after his ownage, Josephus

[1] Josephus Aut. Book II, Chap. V, p. 93.

says that when Moses was nourished in the king's palace he was appointed general of the army against the Ethiopians and conquered them; when he married the king's daughter, because out of her affection for him, she delivered the city up to him. Nor perhaps, did St. Stephen refer to anything else when he said of Moses, before he was sent by God to the Israelites that he was not only learned in all the wisdom of the Egyptians but was also mighty in words and in deeds.[1]

VII.

How Moses Fled out of Egypt Into Midian.

Now the Egyptians after they had been preserved by Moses, entertained a hatred toward him, as suspecting that he would take occasion from his good success to raise a sedition, and bring innovations into Egypt, and told the king he ought to be slain. The king had also some intentions, of himself, to the same purpose and this as well out of envy at his glorious expedition at the head of his army as out of fear of being brought low by him, and being instigated by the sacred scribes, he was ready to undertake to kill Moses. But when he had learned beforehand what plots there were against him he went away privately; and because the public roads were watched, he took his flight through the deserts and where his enemies could not suspect he would travel; and though he was destitute of food he went on and despised that difficulty courageously. And when he came to the city of Midian which lay upon the Red Sea and was so occasion offered him by the custom of the country, of doing what recommended his virtue and afforded him an opportunity of bettering his circumstances.

For that country having but little water, the shepherds

[1] Acts. VII-22 (Whiston).

used to seize on the wells, before others came, lest their flocks should want water, and lest it should be spent by others before they came. There were now, therefore, to this well seven sisters that were virgins, the daughters of Raguel, a priest, and one thought worthy, by the people of the country, of great honor; these virgins who took care of their father's flock, which sort of work it was customary and very familiar for women to do in the country of the Troglodites, they came first of all and drew water out of the well in a quantity sufficient for their flocks, into troughs which were made for the reception of that water. But when the shepherds came upon the maidens and drove them away that they might have the command of the waters themselves, Moses, thinking it would be a terrible reproach upon him if he overlooked the young women under unjust oppression and should suffer the violence of the men to prevail over the right of the maidens, he drove away the men who had a mind to more than their share and afforded a proper assistance to the women who, when they had received such a benefit from him, came to their father and told him how they had been affronted by the shepherds, and assisted by a stranger and entreated that he would not let this generous action be done in vain, nor go without a reward. Now the father took it well from his daughters that they were so desirous to reward their benefactor, and bid them bring Moses into his presence, that he might be rewarded as he deserved. And when Moses came he told him what testimony his daughters bare to him, that he had assisted them; and that as he admired him for his virtue he said that Moses had bestowed such assistance on persons, not insensible of benefits, but where they were both willing and able to return the kindness and even to exceed the measure of his generosity. So he made him his son, and gave him one of his daughters in marriage; (Ex. II–21) and he appointed him to be the guardian and superintendent over his cattle, for of old all the wealth of the barbarians was in those cattle.[1]

So Moses, when he understood that the Pharaoh, in whose reign he fled away was dead, asked leave of Raguel to go to Egypt for the benefit of his own people; and he took with him Zipporah, the daughter of Raguel, whom he had married and the children he had by her, Gersom and Eleazar, and made haste into Egypt.[2]

VIII.

Moses Receives Jethro, his Father-in-Law.

Now when Raguel, Moses's father-in-law understood in what a prosperous condition his affairs were he willingly came to meet him; and Moses took Zipporah, his wife and his children and pleased himself with his coming. And when he had offered sacrifice he made a feast for the multitude near the bush he had formerly seen; which multitude, every one according to their families partook of the feast. But Aaron and his family took Raguel and sang hymns to God as to him who had been the author and procurer of their deliverance and freedom. They also praised their conductor as by him whose virtue it was that all things had succeeded so well with them. Raguel also in his eucharisti-

[1] Josephus, Book II, Chap. XI.
[2] Josephus, Book II, Chap. XIII.

cal oration to Moses, made great encomiums upon the whole multitude; and he could not but admire Moses, for his fortitude and that humanity he had shown in the deliverance of his friends.[1]

The next day as Raguel saw Moses in the midst of a crowd of business, (for he determined the differences of those that referred them to him) everyone still going to him and supposing that they should then only obtain justice, if he were the arbitrator; and those that lost their causes thought it no harm, while they thought they lost them justly and not by partiality. Raguel, however, said nothing to him at the time as not desirous to be any hindrance to such as had a mind to make use of the virtue of their conductor. But afterward he took him to himself and when he had him alone he instructed him in what he ought to do, and advised him to leave the trouble of lesser causes to others, but himself to take care of the greater and of the people's welfare; for that certain others of the Hebrews might be found that were fit to determine causes, but that nobody but a Moses could take care of the safety of so many ten thousands. Be not therefore insensible of thine own virtue and what thou hast done by ministering under God to the people's preservation. Permit, therefore, the determination of common causes to be done by others, but do thou reserve thyself to the attendance on God only; and look out for methods of preserving the multitude from their present distress. Make use of the method I suggest to you as to human affairs, and take a review of the army and appoint chosen rulers over tens of thousands and then over thousands; then divide them into five hun-

[1] Josephus, Book III, Chap. III.

dreds, and again into hundreds and into fifties, and set rulers over each of them, who may distinguish them into thirties and keep them in order, and at last number them by twenties and by tens; and let there be one commander over each number to be denominated from the number of those over whom they are rulers but these such as the whole multitude have tried and do approve as being good and righteous men; and let these rulers decide the controversies they have one with another. But if any great cause arise let them bring the cognizance of it before the rulers of a higher dignity; but if any great difficulty arise that is too hard for even their determination let them send it to thee. By these means two advantages will be gained: that the Hebrews will have justice done and thou wilt be able to attend constantly upon God and procure him to be more favorable to the people.

This was the admonition of Raguel; and Moses received his advice very kindly and acted according to his suggestion. Nor did he conceal the invention of this method nor pretend to it himself, but informed the multitude who it was that invented it, nay, he has named Raguel in the books he wrote as the person who invented this ordering of the people as thinking it right to give true testimony to worthy persons, although he might have gotten reputation by ascribing to himself the inventions of other men.

Whence we may learn the virtuous disposition of Moses.[1]

Note. This manner of electing the judges and officers of the Israelites by the testimonies and suffrages of the people before they were ordained by God or by Moses deserves to be carefully noted because it was the pattern in the like manner of the choice and ordination of Bishops, Presbyters and Deacons in the Christian church. (*Whiston*).

[1] Jos. Book III, Chap. IV.

IX.

The Queen of Sheba.

There was then a woman queen of Egypt and Ethiopia; she was inquisitive into philosophy and one that on other accounts was to be admired. When this queen heard of the virtue and prudence of Solomon, she had a great mind to see him, she being desirous to be satisfied by her own experience and not by bare hearing (for reports thus heard are likely enough to comply with a false opinion while they wholly depend on the credit of the relaters); so she resolved to come to him, and that especially in order to have a trial of his wisdom while she proposed questions of very great difficulty and entreated that he would solve their hidden meaning. Accordingly she came to Jerusalem with rich splendor, and rich furniture; for she brought with camels laden with gold, with several sorts of sweet spices and with precious stones. Now upon the king's kind reception of her, he both showed a great desire to please her, and easily comprehending in his mind the meaning of her curious questions she propounded to him he resolved them sooner than any one could have expected, so she was amazed at the wisdom of Solomon, and discovered that it was more excellent upon trial than what she had heard by report beforehand; and especially she was surprised at the fineness and largeness of his royal palace, and not less at the good order of the apartments for she observed that the king had therein shown great wisdom; but she was beyond measure astonished at the house which was called the forest of Lebanon as also at the magnificence of his daily table, and the circumstances of its preparation and ministration with the apparel of his servants that waited, and the decent management of their attendance nor was she less affected with those daily sacrifices which were offered to God and the careful management which the priests and Levites used about them. When she saw this done every day she was in the greatest admiration imaginable, insomuch that she was not able to contain the surprise she was in, but openly confessed how wonderfully she was affected; for she proceeded to discourse with the king and thereby owned that she was overcome with admiration at the things before related; and said, "all things, indeed O king, that came to our knowledge by report, came with uncertainty as to our belief of them; both such as thou, thyself possessed, I mean wisdom and prudence, and the happiness thou hast from thy kingdom, certainly the fame that came to us was no falsity; it was not only a true report, but it related thy happiness after a much lower manner, than I now see it before my eyes. For as for the report it only attempted to persuade our hearing, but did not so make known the dignity of the things themselves as does the sight of them, and being present among them I indeed, who did not believe what was reported by reason of the multitude and grandeur of the things I inquired about, do see them to be much more numerous, than they were reported to be. Accordingly I esteem the Hebrew people as well as thy servants and friends to be happy, who enjoy thy presence, hear thy wisdom every day, continually. One would therefore bless God who hath so loved this country and those that inhabit therein as to make thee king over them."

Now when the queen had thus demonstrated how deeply the king had affected her, her disposition was known by certain presents, for she gave him twenty talents of gold, and an immense quantity of spices and precious stones. (They say also that we possess the root of that balsam which our country still bears by this woman's gift.) Solomon also repaid her with many good things and principally by bestowing upon her what she chose of her own inclination, for there was nothing she desired which he denied her and as he was very generous and liberal in his own temper so did he show the greatness of his soul in bestowing on her what she herself desired of him.

So when this queen of Ethiopia had obtained what we have already given an account of and had again communicated to the king what she brought with her, she returned to her own kingdom.

X.

Carthage.

Carthage is said to have been founded nearly 900 years before the Christian Era by Dido, with a colony of Tyrians. The government, at first monarchical, became afterwards republican, and it is commended by Aristotle as one of the most perfect of antiquity. The two chief magistrates called suffetes or judges were elected annually from the first families. The religion was a cruel superstition and human victims were offered in sacrifice.

In the time of the Punic wars, Carthage was the most commercial and wealthy city and one of the most splendid in the world. It had under its dominion about 300 smaller towns in Africa bordering on the Mediterranean, a great part of Spain, also of Sicily and other islands. The Carthaginians worked the gold mines of Spain, they were devoted to commerce and had the vices and characteristics of a commercial people. The Romans, who were their rivals and enemies, represented them as wanting in integrity and honor, hence the ironical phrase Punica fides [Punic faith] to denote treachery.

The Periphes, or voyage of Hanuo, an illustrious Carthaginian who wrote an account of his expedition affords proof of ardent enterprise. Carthage produced several celebrated generals, among whom were Hamilcar, Hasdrubal and Hannibal; the last, the most formidable enemy that Rome ever experienced.[1]

The most distinguished Carthaginian commander in the first Punic war was Hamilcar who was the father of Hannibal, and who trained his son to war and made him swear a perpetual enmity to the Roman name. Hannibal was one of the greatest generals of antiquity and at the early age of twenty-six was raised to the command of the Carthaginian army. He commenced the second Punic war by besieging Saguntum, a city of Spain, in alliance with the Romans. After a siege of seven months, the desperate inhabitants set fire to the city and perished in the flames. Hannibal now formed the bold design of carrying the war into Italy and by an arduous and toilsome march he led his army over the Pyrenees and afterwards over the Alps, without halting, one of the most wonderful exploits of which there is any record; and though having lost 30,000 men, rushed into Italy and gained four great victories. The first over Scipio, near the Tici-mus; the second over Sempronions near the Trebia; and the third over Flaminius near the Lake Thrasmenus; and the fourth over Æmilius. Among

[1] Worcester Sec. IV, p. 69.

the slain were 5,000 or 6,000 Roman knights, the greater part of the whole body. The last was the most memorable defeat the Romans ever suffered. According to Livy 50,000 and according to Polybius no less than 70,000 of their troops were left dead upon the field together with the consul Æmilius, and Hannibal is said to have sent to Carthage three bushels of gold rings which they wore on their fingers.

HANNIBAL.

Hannibal has been censured for not making the best of his great victory by immediately attacking Rome, and instead of doing this for leading his troops into winter quarters at Capua where they were corrupted and enervated by dissipation in that luxurious city.

The Romans being now guided by the counsels of the sagacious and prudent Fabius Maximus concentrated their strength.

The chief command of their armies was given to Fabius, styled the shield, and to Marcellus, the sword of Rome. The good fortune of Hannibal now forsook him and he remained 13 years in Italy after the battle of Canne, without gaining any signal advantage. At the siege of Nola was repulsed by Marcellus with considerable loss, and his army was harassed and weakened by Fabius.

Syracuse, which had taken part with Carthage, was besieged by Marcellus and after being defended for three years, by the inventive genius of the celebrated mathematician, Archimedes, it was at last compelled to surrender.

This event put an end to the kingdom of Syracuse, which now became a part of the Roman province of Sicily. A large army of Carthaginians was sent from Spain, into Italy under the command of Asdrubal, the brother of Hannibal, who was defeated with great slaughter by the Romans under the command of the consuls, Livy and Nero, near the small river Metaurus, which empties into the Tyrrhem sea.

Scipio, afterwards surnamed Africanus, having conquered Spain, passed over into Africa, with a Roman army and carried havoc and devastation to the walls of Carthage.

Alarmed for the fate of their empire the Carthaginians immediately recalled Hannibal from Italy. These two great commanders, Hannibal and Scipio at the head of their respective armies fought in the plains of Zama, a memorable battle in which the Carthaginians were totally defeated. A peace soon followed the conditions of which were that Carthage should abandon Spain, Sicily and all the other islands in the Mediterranean, surrender all their prisoners, give up their whole fleet except ten galleys and in future undertake no war without the consent of the Romans. This terminated the second Punic war, in the humiliation of Carthage after having continued for 17 years. Hannibal afterwards fled from his country and passed the last thirteen years of his life in Syria and Bithynia. During his exile, Scipio resided a while in the same country and many friendly conversations passed between them. In one of which the Roman is said to have asked the Carthaginian whom he thought the greatest general, Hannibal immediately replied "Alexander, because that with a small body of men, he had defeated very numerous armies and had overrun a great part of the world." "And who do you think deserves the next place?" continued the Roman. "Pyrrhus" replied the other; "he first taught the method of forming a camp to the best advantage. Nobody knew better how to post guards more properly." "And whom do you place next to those?" said Scipio. "Myself," said Hannibal at which Scipio asked with a smile, "Where then would you have placed yourself if you had conquered me?" "Above Alexander," replied the Carthaginian, "above Pyrrhus and above all other generals."[1]

Hannibal's Treaty.

IV. Treaty concluded between Hannibal, general of the Carthagenians, and Phillip king of Macedonia, in the fourth year of the second Punic war, 215 B. C.[2]

[1] Worcester, Sec. V, p. 72.
[2] From Polyb. II, p. 598; Hieren Ap. p. 483.

This is the treaty which Hannibal the general, Mago, Myrcan, Barmocar and all the senators of Carthage that were with him, and all the Carthaginians that are in the army with him have sworn with Xenophams, the son of Chomachus, the ambassador deputed by king Phillip, the son of Demetrius, in his own name, and in the name of the Macedonians and their allies.

In the presence of Jupiter, Juno and Apollo; in the presence of the deity of the Carthaginians, and of Hercules and Iolaus, in the presence of Mars, Triton, and Poseidon; in the presence of all the gods who are with us in the camp and of the sun, the moon, and the earth; in the presence of the rivers, the lakes, and the waters; in the presence of all the gods who preside over the state of Carthage in the presence of all the gods who preside over the Macedonian empire, and the rest of Greece; in the presence of all the gods who direct the affairs of this war, and who are witnesses of the faith; Hannibal, the general and all the senators of Carthage that are with him and all the Carthaginians that are in the army with him, have said, with the consent of you and of us, this treaty of amity and concord shall connect us together as friends, as kindred, and as brothers upon the following conditions:

King Phillip and the Macedonians, together with the rest of the Greeks that are in alliance with them shall protect and help the people of Carthage, Hannibal the general, and those that are with him; the governors in every place in which the laws of Carthage are observed; the people of Utica, and all the cities and nations that are subject to the Carthaginian sway, together with their armies and their allies; the cities likewise and all the people with whom we are allied, in Italy, in Gaul and in Liguria; and all those that shall hereafter enter into friendship and alliance with us in those countries.

The Carthaginians, on the other hand, the people of Utica and all the other cities and states that are subject to the Carthaginians, with their allies and armies, the cities also and all the people of Italy, of Gaul and of Liguria, that are at this time in alliance with us, and all others likewise that shall hereafter be received into our alliance in any of those parts of Italy; shall protect and defend king Phillip and the Macedonians, together with the rest of the Greeks that are in alliance with them. We will not engage in any ill designs or employ any kind of treachery the one against the other. But with all alacrity and willingness, without any deceit or fraud, you, the Macedonians shall declare yourselves the enemies of those that are enemies of the Carthaginians; those kings alone excepted, and those parts and cities, with which you are connected by any treaty. And we also on the other hand, will be the enemies of those that are enemies of King Phillip; those kings and cities and nations alone excepted, to which we are already bound by treaty. You shall be partners also with us in the war, in which we are now engaged against the Romans; till the gods give to you and to us a happy peace. You shall supply us with the assistance that is requisite, and in the manner that shall be stipulated between us. And if the gods, refusing success to our endeavors, in the war against the Romans and their allies should dispose us to enter into treaty with them, we shall insist, that you also be included in the treaty, and that the peace be made upon these expressed conditions; that the Romans shall at no time make war against us; that they shall not remain masters, Corcyra,

Apollonia, Epidanenus, Pharos, Dimalle and Atintania. And that they shall restore also to Demetrius of Pharos, all the persons of his kindred, who are now detained in public custody at Rome. If the Romans shall afterwards make war either against you or us, we will mutually send such assistance as shall be requisite to either party. The same thing also will we perform if any other power shall declare war against us; those cities and states alone excepted with which we are allied by treaty. If at any time it should be judged expedient to add to the present treaty or to detract from it, it shall be done with mutual consent.

NOTE. Hannibal was at this time in Lower Italy and hoped by this union with Phillip, who was to invade Italy by crossing the Adriatic Sea, to annihilate Rome.

About fifty years after the conclusion of the second Punic war, the Carthaginians attempted to repel the Numidians who made incursions into a territory claimed by the former. The Romans, pretending this was a violation of their treaty laid hold of it as a pretext for commencing the third Punic war, with a determination to effect the entire destruction of Carthage. Porcius Cata, the censor, who now swayed the decisions of the senate, had long cherished this savage design and had been in the habit of concluding his speeches with this expression "Delenda est Carthage," "Carthage must be destroyed."

The Carthaginians conscious of their inability to resist the Romans offered every submission and were ready to acknowledge themselves subjects of Rome. They yielded up to the Romans, their ships, their arms, and munitions of war. They were then required to abandon the city in order that it might be destroyed.

This demand was heard by the inhabitants with a mixed feeling of indignation and despair; but the spirit of liberty and independence not being yet extinct they were roused to make the most strenuous effort, having resolved to sacrifice their lives rather than to obey the barbarous mandate.

After the most desperate resistance for three years, the city was at last taken by Scipio, the second Africanus, and being set on fire, the flames continued to rage during 17 days. Thus was Carthage with its walls and buildings razed to its foundations. Such of the inhabitants as disdained to surrender themselves prisoners of war were either massacred or perished in the flames. The scenes of horror were such as to force tears even from the Roman general.

A new Carthage arose from its ruins, with the title of a colony; and though Carthage might yield to the royal perogative of Constantinople and perhaps to the trade of Alexandria or the splendor of Antioch, she still maintained the second rank in the West; as the Rome of the African world.

That wealthy and opulent metropolis displayed in a dependent condition the image of a flourishing republic. Carthage contained the manufactures, the arms and the treasures of the six provinces. A regular subordination of civil honors, gradually ascended from the chief procurators of streets and quarters of the city to the tribunal of the supreme magistrate, who with the title of proconsul, represented the state dignity of a consul of ancient Rome. Schools and gymnasia were instituted for the education of the African youth; and the liberal arts and manners, grammar, rhetoric and philosophy were publicly taught in the Greek and Latin languages. The buildings of Carthage were uniform and magnificent. A shady grove was planted in the midst of the capital, the new port, a secure and capacious harbor was subservient to the commercial industry of citizens and strangers; and the splendid games of the circus and theatre were exhibited almost in the presence of the barbarians.

The reputation of the Carthaginians was not equal to that of their country and the reproach of Punic faith still adhered to their subtle and faithless character. The habits of trade and the abuse of luxury had corrupted their manners. In 439 A. D. they were surprised by the Vandals and reduced to a state of servitude.[1]

XI.

SEPTIMUS SEVERUS. (NEGRO EMPEROR OF ROME).

From Gibbon's Decline and Fall of the Roman Empire.

Chapter V.

The country of Pannonia and Dalmatia which occupied the space between the Danube and the Hadriatic was one of the last and most difficult conquests of the Romans. In the defence of national freedom two hundred thousand of the barbarians had once appeared in the field, alarmed the declining age of Augustus and exercised the vigilant prudence of Tiberius at the head of the collected force of the Empire. The Pannonians yielded at length to the arms and institutions of Rome.

[1] Gibbon's Rome, p. 259.

Their recent subjection, however, the neighborhood and even the mixture of the unconquered tribes and perhaps the climate adapted as it has been observed, to the production of great bodies and slow minds all contributed to preserve some remains of their original ferocity and under the tame and uniform countenance of Roman provincials the hardy features of the natives were still to be discerned. Their warlike youth afforded an inexhaustible supply of recruits to the legions stationed on the banks of the Danube and which from a perpetual warfare against the Germans and Samartians were deservedly esteemed the best troops in the service.

The Pannonian army was at this time commanded by Septimus Severus, a native African, who in the gradual ascent of private honors had concealed his daring ambition, which was never diverted from its steady course by the allurements of pleasure, the apprehension of danger or the feelings of humanity. On the first news of the murder of Pertinax he assembled his troops painted in the most lively colors, the crime, the insolence and the weakness of the Praetorian Guards, and animated the legions to arms and to revenge. He concluded, and the peroration was thought extremely eloquent, with promising every soldier about four hundred pounds; an honorable donative double in value to the infamous bribe with which Julian had purchased the empire. The acclamations of the army immediately saluted Severus, with the names of Augustus Pertinax and Emperor and he (A. D. 193 April 13th) thus attained the lofty station to which he was invited by conscious merit, and a long train of dreams and omens, the fruitful offspring either of his superstition or policy.

The new candidate for empire saw and improved the

peculiar advantage of his situation. His province extended to the Julian Alps which gave an easy access into Italy; and he remembered the saying of Augustus that a Pannonian army might in ten days appear in sight of Rome, by a celerity proportioned to the greatness of the occasion he might reasonably hope to revenge Pertinax, punish Julian and receive the homage of the senate and people as their lawful emperor, before his competitors, separated from Italy by a vast tract of sea and land, were apprised of his success or even of his election. During the whole expedition he scarcely allowed himself any moments for food or sleep; marching on foot and in complete armor at the head of his columns he insinuated himself into the confidence and affection of his troops pressed their diligence, revived their spirits, animated their hopes and was well satisfied to share the hardships of the meanest soldier whilst he kept in view the infinite superiority of his reward.

The wretched Julian had thought himself prepared to dispute the empire with the governor of Syria but in the invincible and rapid approach of the Pannonian legions he saw his inevitable ruin. The hasty arrival of every messenger increased his just apprehensions. He was successively informed that Severus had passed the Alps; that the Italian cities unwilling or unable to oppose his progress had received him with the warmest professions of joy and duty; that the important place of Ravenna had surrendered without resistance and that the Hadriatic fleet was in the hands of the conqueror. The enemy was now within two hundred and fifty miles of Rome; and every moment diminished the narrow span, life and empire allotted Julian.

He attempted, however, to prevent or at least to protract his ruin. He implored the venal faith of the

Praetorians, filled the city with unavailing preparations for war; drew lines round the suburbs and even strengthened the fortifications of the palace; as if those last intrenchments could be defended without hope of relief against a victorious invader. Fear and shame prevented the guards from deserting his standard; but they trembled at the name of Pannonian legions, commanded by an experienced general and accustomed to vanquish the barbarians on the frozen Danube. They quitted with a sigh the pleasures of the baths and theatres to put on arms whose use they had almost forgotten and beneath the weight of which they were oppressed. The unpractised elephants whose uncouth appearance it was hoped would strike terror into the army of the north threw their unskillful riders; and the awkward evolutions of the marines, drawn from the fleet of Misenum were an object of ridicule to the populace; whilst the Senate enjoyed with secret pleasure the distress and weakness of the usurper.

Every motion of Julian betrayed his trembling perplexity. He insisted that Severus should be declared a public enemy by the senate. He intreated that the Pannonian general might be associated to the empire. He sent public ambassadors to negotiate with his rival; he dispatched private assassins to take away his life. He designed that the Vestal Virgins and all the colleges of priests in the sacerdotal habits and bearing before them the sacred pledges of the Roman religion, should advance in solemn procession to meet the Pannonian legions and at the same time he vainly tried to interrogate, or to appease the fates, by magic ceremonies and unlawful sacrifices.[1]

[1] Hist. August p. 62–63.

Severus who dreaded neither his arms nor his enchantments guarded himself from the only danger of secret conspiracy, by the faithful attendance of six hundred chosen men, who never quitted his person or their cuirrasses either by night or by day during the whole march. Advancing with a steady and rapid course he passed without difficulty the defiles of the Apennine, received into his party the troops and ambassadors sent to retard his progress and made a short halt at Interamia about seventy miles from Rome. His victory was already secure; but the despair of the Praetorians might have rendered it bloody; and Severus had the laudable ambition of ascending the throne without drawing the sword. His emissaries dispersed in the capital, assured the guards, that provided they would abandon their worthless prince and the perpetrators of the murder of Pertinax, to the justice of the conqueror, he would no longer consider that melancholy event as the act of the whole body. The faithless Praetorians whose resistance was supported only by sullen obstinacy, gladly complied with the easy conditions, seized the greatest part of the assassins and signified to the senate that they no longer defended the cause of Julian. That assembly convoked by the consul unanimously acknowledged Severus as lawful emperor, decreed divine honors to Pertinax and pronounced a sentence of deposition and death against his unfortunate successor. Julian was conducted into a private apartment of the baths of the palace (A. D. 193, June 2) beheaded as a common criminal after having purchased with an immense treasure an anxious and precarious reign of only sixty-six days.[1]

[1] Dion. LXXIII, p. 1240. Herodian III, p. 83. Hist. August, p. 63.

Severus covered a distance of eight hundred miles in forty days or twenty miles a day without halt or intermission. The almost incredible expedition of Severus, who in so short a space of time, conducted a numerous army from the banks of the Danube to those of the Tyber, proves at once the plenty of provisions produced by agriculture and commerce, the goodness of roads, the discipline of the legions and the indolent, subdued temper of the provinces.

The first cares of Severus were bestowed on two measures, the one dictated by policy, the other by decency; the revenge and the honors due to the memory of Pertinax. Before the new emperor entered Rome he issued his commands to the Praetorian Guards directing them to wait his arrival on a large plain near the city, without arms but in the habits of ceremony in which they were accustomed to attend their sovereign. He was obeyed by those haughty troops, whose contrition was the effect of their just terrors. A chosen part of the Illyrian army encompassed them with levelled spears. Incapable of flight or resistance they expected their fate in silent consternation. Severus mounted the tribunal, sternly reproached them with perfidy and cowardice, dismissed them with ignominy from the trust which they had betrayed, despoiled of their splendid ornaments, and banished them upon pain of death, to the distance of a hundred miles from the capital. During the transaction another detachment had been sent to seize their arms, occupy their camp and prevent the hasty consequences of their despair.[1]

The funeral and consecration of Pertinax was next solemnized with every circumstance of sad magnificence.

[1] Dion I. LXXIV, p. 1241. Herodian I. II, p. 84.

The senate with a melancholy pleasure, performed the last rites to excellent prince, whom they had loved and still regretted. The concern of his successor was probably less sincere. He esteemed the virtues of Pertinax but those virtues would forever have confined his ambition to a private station. Severus pronounced his funeral oration, with studied eloquence, inward satisfaction and well acted sorrow; and by this pious regard to his memory convinced the credulous multitude that he alone was worthy to supply his place. Sensible, however, that arms, not ceremony must assert his claim to the empire, he left Rome at the end of thirty days, and without suffering himself to be elated by this easy victory prepared to encounter his more formidable rivals.

The uncommon abilities and fortune of Severus have induced an elegant historian to compare him with the first and greatest of the Caesars.[1]

In less than four years (A. D. 193–197) Severus subdued the riches of the east and the valor of the west. He vanquished two competitors of reputation and ability and defeated numerous armies, provided with weapons and discipline equal to his own. In that age the art of fortification and the principles of tactics were well understood by all the Roman generals; and the constant superiority of Severus was that of an artist who uses the same instruments with more skill and industry than his rivals. I shall not, however, enter into a minute narrative of these operations; but as the two civil wars against Niger and against Albiuns were almost the same in their conduct, event and consequences, I shall collect into one point of view the most striking circumstances,

[1] Herodias, 1. III, p. 112.

tending to develop the character of the conqueror and the state of the empire.

Falsehood and insincerity, unsuitable as they seem to the dignity of public transactions offend us with a less degrading idea of meanness, than when they are found in the intercourse of private life. In the latter they discover a want of courage; in the other only a defect of power; and as it is impossible for the most able statesman to subdue millions of followers and enemies by their own personal strength, the world, under the name, policy, seems to have granted them a very liberal indulgence of craft and dissimulation. Yet the arts of Severus cannot be justified by the most ample privileges of state reason. He promised only to betray, he flattered only to ruin and however he might occasionally bind himself by oaths and treaties, his conscience, obsequious to his interest, always released him from the inconvenient obligation.[1]

If his two competitors reconciled by their common danger had advanced upon him without delay, perhaps Severus would have sunk under their united effort. Had they even attacked him at the same time with separate views and separate armies the contest might have been long and doubtful. But they fell singly and successively an easy prey to the arts as well as arms of Severus, of the subtle enemy lulled into security by the moderation of his professions and overwhelmed by the rapidity of his action. He first marched against Niger whose reputation and power he most dreaded but he declined any hostile declaration, suppressed the name of his antagonist and only signified to the senate and the

[1] Herodian I. p. 85.

people his intention of regulating the eastern provinces. In private, he spoke of Niger, his old friend, an intended successor with the most affectionate regard and highly applauded his generous design of revenging the murder of Pertinax. To punish the vile usurper of the throne was the duty of every Roman general. To persevere in arms and to resist a lawful emperor acknowledged by the senate would alone render him criminal.[1]

The sons of Niger had fallen into his hands among the children of the provincial governors, detained at Rome as pledges for the loyalty of their parents. As long as the power of Niger inspired terror or even respect they were educated with the most tender care with the children of Severus himself, even in the letter, in which he announced his victory over Niger, he styles Albinus, the brother of his soul and empire, sends him the affectionate salutations of his wife Julia, and his young family and intreats him to preserve the armies and the republic faithful to their common interest. The messengers charged with this letter were instructed to accost the Caesar with respect to desire a private audience and to plunge their daggers into his heart. The conspiracy was discovered and the too credulous Albinus at length passed over to the continent and prepared for an unequal contest with his rival who rushed upon him at the head of a veteran and victorious army.

The military labors of Severus seem inadequate to the importance of his conquests. Two engagements, the one near the Hellespont, the other in the narrow defiles of Cilicia decided the fate of his Syrian competitor; and the troops of Europe asserted their usual

[1] Hist. August. p. 65.

ascendant over the effeminate natives of Asia. The battle of Lyons where one hundred and fifty thousand (Dion I. LXXV, p. 1260) Romans were engaged was equally fatal to Albinus. The valor of the British army maintained a sharp and doubtful contest with the hardy discipline of the Illyrian legions. The fame and person of Severus appeared during a few moments irrecoverably lost till that war-like prince rallied his fainting troops and led them on to a decisive victory. The war was finished by that memorable day.

Both Niger and Albinus were discovered and put to death in their flight from the field of battle. Their fate excited neither surprise nor compassion. They had staked their lives against the chance of empire and suffered what they would have inflicted; nor did Severus claim the arrogant superiority of suffering his rivals to live in a private station. But his unforgiving temper stimulated by avarice indulged a spirit of revenge where there was no room for apprehension. The most considerable of the provincials, who without any dislike to the fortunate candidate, had obeyed the governor under whose authority they were accidentally placed, were punished by death, exile and especially by the confiscation of their estates. Many cities of the east were stript of their ancient honors and obliged to pay into the treasury of Severus, four times the amount of the sums contributed by them for the service of Niger.[1]

Till the final decision of the war the cruelty of Severus was in some measure restrained by the uncertainty of the event, and his pretended reverence for the senate. The head of Albinus accompanied with a menacing

[1] Dion. I. XXIV, p. 1250.

letter, announced to the Romans, that he was resolved to spare none of the adherents of his unfortunate competitors. He was irritated by the just suspicion that he had never possessed the affection of the senate and he concealed his old malevolence under the discovery of some treasonable correspondences. Thirty-five senators, however, accused of having favored the party of Albinus, he freely pardoned; and, by his subsequent behavior endeavored to convince them, that he had forgotten as well as forgiven their supposed offences. But at the same time he condemned forty-one other senators whose names history has recorded; their wives, children and clients attended them in death and the noblest provincials of Spain and Gaul were involved in the same ruin.

Such rigid justice, for so he termed it, was in the opinion of Severus, the only conduct capable of insuring peace to the people or stability to the prince; and he condescended slightly to lament that to be mild, it was necessary that he should first be cruel (Aurelins Victor). The true interest of an absolute monarch generally coincides with that of his people. Their numbers, their wealth, their order and their security, are the best and only foundations of his royal greatness; and were he totally devoid of virtue, prudence might supply its place and would dictate the same rule of conduct. Severus considered the Roman empire as his property and had no sooner secured possession of it, than he bestowed his care, on the cultivation and improvement of so valuable an acquisition. Salutary laws, executed with inflexible firmness soon corrected most of the abuses with which since the death of Marcus, every part of the government had been infected. In the administration of justice, the judgments of the emperor were characterized by attention, discernment, and impartiality; and whenever he deviated from the strict line of equity it was generally in favor of the poor and oppressed; not so much indeed from a sense of humanity as from the natural propensity of a despot to humble the pride of the rich and to sink all his subjects to the same common level of absolute dependence. His expensive taste for building and magnificent shows, and above all a constant and liberal distribution of corn and provisions, were the surest means of captivating the affection of the Roman people. The misfortunes of civil discord were obliterated. The calm of peace and prosperity was once more experienced in the provinces, and many cities restored by the munificence of Severus assumed the title of his colonies, and attested by public monuments their gratitude and felicity.

The fame of the Roman arms was revived by that warlike emperor and he boasted with a just pride that having received the empire oppressed with foreign and domestic wars, ***he left it established in profound universal and honorable peace.***

Although the wounds of civil war appeared completely healed, its mortal poison still lurked in the vitals of the constitution. Severus possessed a considerable share of vigor and ability; but the daring soul of the first Caesar, or the deep policy of Augustus, were scarcely equal to the task of curbing the insolence of the victorious legions. By gratitude, by misguided policy, by seeming necessity, Severus was induced to relax the nerves of discipline.[1] The vanity of his soldiers was flattered with honor of wearing gold rings; their ease was indulged in the permission

[1] Herodian I. III, p. 115. Hist. August, p. 68.

of living with their wives in the idleness of quarters. He increased their pay beyond the example of former times and taught to expect and soon to claim extraordinary donations on every public occasion of danger or festivity. Elated by success, enervated by luxury, and raised above the level of subjects by their dangerous privileges they soon became incapable of military fatigue, oppressive to the country, and impatient of a just subordination. Their officers asserted the superiority of rank by a more profuse and elegant luxury.

There is still extant a letter of Severus lamenting the licentious state of the army and exhorting one of his generals to begin the necessary reformation, from the tribunes themselves; since he justly observes the officer who has forfeited the esteem, will never command the obedience of his soldiers.[1]

Had the emperor pursued the train of reflection he would have discovered that the primary cause of this general corruption might be ascribed not indeed to the example but to the pernicious indulgence, however, of the commander-in-chief.

The Praetorians who murdered their emperor and sold the empire had received the just punishment of their treason; but the necessary though dangerous institution of guards was soon restored on a new model by Severus and increased to four times the ancient numbers.[2]

Formerly these troops had recruited in Italy; and as the adjacent provinces gradually imbibed the softer manners of Rome, the levies were extended to Macedonia,

[1] Hist. August, p. 73.
[2] Herodian l. III, p. 131.

Noricum, and Spain. In the room of these elegant troops, better adapted to the pomp of courts than to the uses of war, it was established by Severus that from all the legions of the frontiers, the soldiers most distinguished for strength, valor, and fidelity should be occasionally draughted and promoted, as an honor and reward, into the more eligible service of the guards. *Dion. I. XXV, p. 1243.* By this new institution, the Italian youths were diverted from the exercise of arms and the capital was terrified by the strange aspect and manners of a multitude of barbarians. But Severus flattered himself that the legions would consider these chosen Praetorians as the representatives of the whole military order; and that the present aid of fifty thousand men, superior in arms and appointments to any force that could be brought into the field against them would forever crush the hopes of rebellion, and secure the empire to himself and his posterity.

The command of these favored and formidable troops became the first office of the empire. As the government degenerated into military despotism, the Praetorian Praefect, who in his origin had been a simple captain of the guards, was placed not only at the head of the army, but of the finances and even of the law. In every department of administration he represented the person and exercised the authority of the emperor. The first Praefect who enjoyed and abused this immense power was Plantianus, the favorite minister of Severus. His reign lasted about ten years, till the marriage of his daughter with the eldest son of the emperor, which seemed to assure his fortune, proved the occasion of his ruin. The animosities of the palace by irritating the ambition and alarming the fears of Plantianus threatened to produce a revolution and obliged the emperor who still loved him to consent with reluctance to his death. After the fall of Plantianusan, eminent lawyer, Paupinian was appointed to execute the motley office of Praetorian Praefect.

Till the reign of Severus the virtue and even the good sense of the emperors had been distinguished by their zeal or affected reverence for the senate and by a tender regard to the nice frame of civil policy instituted by Augustus. But the youth of Severus had been trained in the implicit obedience of camps and his riper years, spent in the despotism of militarv commands.

His haughty and inflexible spirit could not discover or would not acknowledge, the advantage of preserving an immediate power, however imaginary between the emperor and the army. He disdained to profess himself the servant of an assembly that detested his person and trembled at his frown. He issued his commands, where his request would have proved as effectual, assumed the conduct and style of a sovereign and conqueror and exercised without disguise the whole legislative, as well as executive power. The victory over the senate was easy and inglorious. Every eye and every passion were directed to the supreme magistrate, who possessed the arms and treasure of the state; whilst the senate neither elected by the people nor guarded by military force, nor animated by public spirit rested its declining authority on the frail and crumbling basis of ancient opinion. The fine theory of a republic insensibly vanished and made way for the more natural and substantial feelings of monarchy. As the freedom and honors of Rome were successively communicated to the provinces in which the old government had been either unknown or remembered with abhorrence, the tradition of republican maxims was gradually obliterated.

The Greek historians of the age of the Automines observe with a malicious pleasure, that although the sovereign of Rome in compliance with an obsolete prejudice abstained from the name of king, he possessed the full measure of regal power.

In the reign of Severus the senate was filled with polished and eloquent slaves from the Eastern provinces who justified personal flattery by speculative principles of servitude. These new advocates of prerogative were heard with pleasure by the court and with patience by the people, when they inculcated passive obedience and descanted on the inevitable mischiefs of freedom.

The lawyers and historians concurred in teaching that the imperial authority was held not by the delegated commission but by the irrevocable resignation of the senate; that the emperor was freed from the restraint of civil laws, could command by his arbitrary will the lives and fortunes of his subjects and might dispose of the empire as of his private patrimony. The most eminent of the civil lawyers, and particularly Paupinian, Paulus, and Illpian flourished under the house of Severus; and the Roman jurisprudence having closely united itself with the system of monarchy was supposed to have attained its full maturity and prerogative. The contemporaries of Severus in the enjoyment of peace and glory of his reign, forgave the cruelties by which it had been introduced. Posterity who experienced the fatal effects of the maxims and example justly considered him as the principal author of the decline of the Roman empire.

The ascent to greatness, however steep and dangerous,

may entertain an active spirit with the consciousness and exercise of its own powers; but the possession of a throne could never yet afford a lasting satisfaction to an ambitious mind. This melancholy truth was felt and acknowledged by Severus. Fortune and merit had from a humble station elevated him to the first of mankind. "He had been all things as he said himself and all was of little value."[1]

"Omnia fin et nihil expedit." Oppressed with age and infirmities, careless of fame distracted with the care, not of acquiring but preserving an empire (Dion. Cassins 1. LXXVI, p. 1284), and satiated with power, all his prospects of life were closed. The desire of perpetuating the greatness of his family was the only remaining wish of his ambition and paternal tenderness. Like most of the Africans Severus was passionately addicted to the vain studies of magic and devination, deeply versed in the interpretation of dreams and omens, and perfectly acquainted with the science of judicial astrology; which in almost every age except the present has maintained its dominion over the mind of man.

He had lost his first wife, whilst he was governor of Lionnese Gaul. In the choice of a second, he sought only to connect himself with some favorite of fortune; and as soon as he discovered that a young lady of Enusa in Syria had a royal nativity he solicited and obtained her hand (Hist. August, p. 65). Julia Domna, for that was her name, deserved all that the stars could promise her. She possessed even in advanced age the attractions of beauty (Hist. August, p. 85) and

[1] Hist. August, p. 71.

united to a lively imagination, a firmness of mind and strength of judgment seldom bestowed on her sex. Her amiable qualities never made any deep impression on the dark and jealous temper of her husband; but in her son's reign, she administered the principal affairs of the empire with a prudence that supported his authority; and with a moderation that sometimes corrected his wild extravagances. (Dion. Cassins 1. LXXVII. p. 13, 14.) Julia applied herself to letters and philosophy with some success and with the most splendid reputation. She was the patroness of every art and the friend of every man of genius. The grateful flattery of the learned has celebrated her virtue; but, if we may credit the scandal of ancient history, chastity was very far from being her most conspicuous virtue.[1]

Two sons Caracalla and Geta were the fruit of this marriage and the destined heirs of the empire. The fond hopes of the father and the Roman world, were soon disappointed by these vain youths, who displayed the indolent security of hereditary princes; and a presumption that fortune would supply the place of merit and application. Without any emulation or virtue or talents, they discovered almost from their infancy a fixed and implacable antipathy for each other. Their aversion confirmed by years and fomented by the arts of their interested favorites broke out in childish and gradually in more serious competition; and at length divided the theatre, the circus and the court into two factions actuated by the hopes and fears of their respective leaders. The prudent emperor endeavored by every expedient of advice and authority to allay

[1] Dion. 1. LXXVI, p. 1285 Aurelius Victor.

this growing animosity. The unhappy discord of his sons clouded all his prospects and threatened to overturn a throne raised with so much labor and cemented with so much blood and guarded with every defence of of arms and treasure. With an impartial hand he maintained between them the exact balance of favor conferred on both the rank of Augustus with the revered name of Antonius; and for the first time the Roman world beheld three emperors. Yet even this equal conduct served only to inflame the contest. Whilst the fierce Caracalla asserted the right of primogeniture, the milder Geta courted the affections of the people and the soldiers. In the anguish of a disappointed father Serverus foretold that the weaker of his sons would fall a sacrifice to the stronger; who in his turn would be ruined by his own vices.

In these circumstances the intelligence of a war in Britain and of an invasion (A. D. 208) of the province by the barbarians of the North was received with pleasure by Severus. Though the vigilance of his lieutenants might have been sufficient to repel the distant enemy, he resolved to embrace the honorable pretext of withdrawing his sons from the luxury of Rome which enervated their minds and irritated their passions and of inuring their youth to the toils of war and government. Notwithstanding his advanced age, for he was above three score, and his gout which obliged him to be carried in a litter, he transported himself in person into that remote island attended by his two sons, his whole court and a formidable army. He immediately passed the walls of Hadrian and Antonius and entered the enemy's country with a design of completing the long attempted conquest of Britain. He penetrated to the northern extremity of the island without meeting an enemy. But the concealed ambuscades of the Caledonians who hung unseen on the rear and flanks of his army, the coldness of the climate and the severity of a winter march across the hills and morasses of Scotland are reported to have cost the Romans above fifty thousand men. The Caledonians at length yielded to the powerful and obstinate attack, sued for peace, and surrendered a part of their arms and a large tract of territory.

But their apparent submission lasted no longer than their present terror. As soon as the Roman legions had retired they resumed their hostile independence. Their restless spirit provoked Severus to send a new army into Caledonia with the most bloody orders, not to subdue but to extirpate the natives. They were saved by the death of their haughty enemy.[1]

The Caledonian war, neither marked by decisive events nor attended with any important consequences, would ill deserve our attention; but it is supposed not without a considerable degree of probability that the invasion of Severus is connected with the most shining period of the British history of fable.

The declining health and last illness of Severus inflamed the wild amibtion and black passions of Caracallas's soul. Impatient of any delay or division of empire he attempted more than once to shorten the small remainder of his father's days, and endeavored but without success to excite a mutiny among the troops.[2]

The old emperor had often censured the misguided leniency of Marcus, who by a single act of justice might

[1] Dion. 1. XXVI, p. 1280 Herodian, 1. III, p. 132 etc.
[2] Dion. 1. XXVI, p. 1282, Hist. August, p. 71, Aurelius Victor.

have saved the Romans from the tyranny of his worthless sons. Placed in the same situation, he experienced how easily the rigour of a judge dissolves away in the tenderness of a father. He deliberated, he threatened, but he could not punish; and this last and only instance of mercy was more fatal to the empire than a long series of cruelty.[1]

The disorder of his mind irritated the pains of his body; he wished impatiently for death and hastened the instant of it by his impatience. He expired A. D. 211, Feb. 4 at York in the sixty-fifth year of his life and the eighteenth of a glorious and successful reign.

Caracalla, Roman Emperor 211–17 A. D.

Caracalla, eldest son of Septimus Severus, was born at Lyons 188 A. D. He was originally named Bassianus from his maternal grandfather, but his legal name as it appears on medals and inscriptions was M. Aurelius Antonius. He was nicknamed Caracalla from the long hooded tunic which he wore after the fashion and in the language of the Gauls. He ascended the throne as co-regent with his brother Publius Septimus Antonius Geta whom he afterwards murdered in his mother's arms. His reign was a long train of cruelties. He put to death all the friends and adherents of Geta among them the eminent jurist, Papinianus. He resorted to every possible means to maintain his extravagances and to pay his soldiers. In his famous constitution he bestowed Roman citizenship on all his free subjects not citizens who formed the majority, especially in the

[1] Dion 1. XXVI, p. 1283. Hist. August, p. 89.

provinces but simply in order to levy a greater amount of taxes on releases and heritages, which were paid only by citizens. After almost exhausting Italy by his extortions his arts of oppression were directed against the provinces which had been in a great measure spared by former emperors. In 214 he visited Gaul, Germany, Dacia and Thrace, and after a campaign against the Alemanui assumed the surname of Alemanuicus. He was assassinated at the instigation of Macrinus, prefect of the Praetorians, by one of his veterans named Martialis on the 8th of April, 217, on the way from Edessa to Carrhae.

A people without history, a country, or a flag would be a most extraordinary circumstance yet owing to misplaced facts it is in this light the Negro is regarded. The day has come, however, for a fixed Negro status and this must necessarily be based upon ancestry.

Ambitions and aspirations are inspired largely by pride in our ancestors. Owing to a lack of knowledge or source of information easily accessible we have remained in ignorance to a great extent of the history of Negro peoples. The average school history contains little or nothing, leaving the Negro youth in the darkness of despair.

To-day things are assuming a new aspect and in order to meet the new issues we must needs have an enlarged vision. The narrow confines which have so long held us have been outgrown.

Descendants of kings and princes and illustrious personages we have been denied the smallest item of of their achievements, reciting ever and anon the glories of other races, yet always craving tangible assurance of our own origin. If this little volume of sketches tends in any way to allay this longing we shall feel well paid for our effort.

FINIS

A Select List of Black Classic Press Titles

The Negro

W. E. B. DuBois

Originally published in 1915, Dr. W. E. Burghardt Du Bois' "little book," as he called it, was one of the most important and seminal works on African and African American history. It was small in size but gigantic in purpose. In it Du Bois, unquestionably an eminent historian, brilliantly attempted to encapsulate the ten thousand-year record of the peoples of Africa, then referred to as "Negroes." Introduction by W. Burghardt Turner and Joyce Moore Turner.
ISBN 1-58073-032-9. 1915*, 2004. 281 pp. Paper $14.95.

David Walker's Appeal

David Walker

Walker's Appeal represents one of the earliest African-centered discourses on an oppressed people's right to freedom. African American political philosophy has evolved from many of the themes that it articulates.
ISBN 0-933121-38-5. 1929*, 1993. 108 pp. Paper $8.95.

A Tropical Dependency

Flora Shaw Lugard

When Lady Lugard sat down to write *A Tropical Dependency*, it was not her intention to inspire generations of Africans to regain the independence of their countries. Lugard writes of slavery as though it was a God-given right of Europeans to own Africans as slaves. Ironically, her text on Africa's place in history reaffirms the belief that "If Africa did it once, Africa can do it again!" Introduction by John Henrik Clarke.
ISBN 0-933121-92-X. 1906*, 1997. 508 pp. Paper $24.95.

The Name "Negro": Its Origin and Evil Use

Richard B. Moore

Moore's study focuses on the exploitive nature of the word "Negro." Connecting its origins to the African Slave Trade, he shows how the label "Negro" was used to separate African descendants and to confirm their supposed inferiority.
ISBN 0-933121-35-0. 1960*, 1992. 108 pp. Paper $10.95.

Wonderful Ethiopians of the Ancient Cushite Empire

Drusilla Dunjee Houston

Mrs. Houston describes the origin of civilization and establishes links among the ancient Black populations of Arabia, Persia, Babylonia, and India. In each case, she concludes that the ancient Blacks who inhabited these areas were all culturally related.
ISBN 0-933121-01-6. 1926*, 1985. 280 pp. Paper $14.95.

The Exiles of Florida

Joshua R. Giddings

During the early part of the nineteenth century, the United States conducted a bruta campaign to re-enslave Blacks who escaped slavery and found freedom in Nativ American settlements in Florida. Giddings' observations document the struggl waged by these brave Africans and their Native American hosts.
ISBN 0-933121-47-4. 1858*, 1997. 338 pp. Paper $16.95.

Ancient Egypt the Light of the World

Gerald Massey

An epic analysis of ancient origins and beliefs, this first volume of Ancient Egyp elaborates how the first humans, who emerged in Africa, created thought. In th second volume Massey examines the Precession of the Equinoxes and the ol Kamite sources of Christianity.
ISBN 0-933121-31-8. 1907*, 1992. 944 pp. Paper $59.95.

A Book of the Beginnings

Gerald Massey

In volume one, Massey focuses on Egyptian origins in the British Isles. In th second volume, he explores the African/Egyptian roots of the Hebrews, th Akkado-Assyrians, and the Maori. By linking these diverse cultures and origins t their African roots, Massey demonstrates not only the extent of African influenc but its durability as well.
ISBN 0-933121-93-8. 1881*, 1995. 1200 pp. Two volume set. Cloth $84.95.

The Natural Genesis

Gerald Massey

By centralizing Egypt as the root of Western civilization's myths, symbols religions, and languages, this famed Egyptologist and 'mythographer' challenge conventions of theology as well as fundamental notions of race supremacy. Introduction by Dr. Charles S. Finch.
ISBN 1-57478-009-3. 1883*, 1998. 1087 pp. Two volume set. Paper $59.95.

Christianity, Islam and the Negro Race

Edward W. Blyden

Blyden offers an early African-centered perspective on race, religion, and the development of Africa.
ISBN 0-933121-41-5. 1887*, 1993. 441 pp. Paper $14.95.

To order, send a check or money order to:
Black Classic Press
P.O. Box 13414
Baltimore, MD 21203-3414

Include $5 for shipping and handling, and $.50 for each additional book ordered. Credit card orders call: 1-800-476-8870

For a complete list of titles, please visit our website at www.blackclassic.com

**Indicates first year published*

180718-200-